WHAT DID JESUS ASK?

WHAT
DID JESUS
ASK

CHRISTIAN LEADERS
REFLECT ON HIS QUESTIONS
OF FAITH

EDITED BY ELIZABETH DIAS

FOREWORD BY NANCY GIBBS

Editor, TIME magazine

TIME
Books

CONTENTS

NANCY GIBBS

FOREWORD

This book was born of a conversation between a journalist and a surgeon—people, you might say, for whom questions matter. The doctor looking to diagnose, the journalist looking to discover, believe that in the strength and sharpness of the question lies the possibility of a meaningful answer, one that shines light or breaks ground. I can't remember when it was that my friend Dr. Scott Haig first raised the topic of the questions Jesus asked, but I remember being intrigued, particularly since in this case the questions are of a wholly different nature. On the one hand, people of free will can answer them any way they choose; on the other, an all-knowing God already knows the answer. So why ask?

"Why ask?" is a question about questions, and that is the theme this book explores, through the eyes, insights and experiences of more than 70 theologians from many schools of Christianity. Perhaps we reflexively associate teachers and preachers with answers when we should really think about questions. The best teachers treat interrogation as navigation, holding back the shortcuts and letting the listeners explore so that upon arrival at an answer, they've brought the muscles built by the journey.

Put Jesus on a grassy mountainside or in a boat just off the beach with thousands of listeners and he preached: stories and parables, announcements, warnings. But listen to him talking with those closest to him and what we hear are questions. Yes, he was the son of a culture that talked like that, questions answered with better questions, which stymied critics and inspired disciples. But Jesus was neither an academic nor given to argument for its own sake. His mission was to give, some say to be, an answer.

Throughout his life, Jesus used questions to show people who he was. The earliest question comes from a curiously nonplussed little boy, lost for three days in a teeming city, to the frantic mother who had just found him in the temple.

"Why were you searching for me?" Jesus asks Mary. "Didn't you know I had to be in my Father's house?"

She obviously didn't. But Mary and the many who loved him soon learned why from this and the many other questions, and answers, that Jesus spoke. His questions, like the parables, fly under our mental radar and right in, "dividing bones and marrow," challenging us not just to answer but to ask why the question needed to be posed at all.

Sometimes the question answers itself: "You of little faith, why are you so afraid?" (Mathew 8:26). Sometimes the question *is* the answer—particularly the last, agonizing one from the Cross, asked of God himself: "My God, my God, why have you forsaken me?" This final question, when Jesus expresses those most human of spiritual conditions—fear, doubt, loneliness—goes to the heart of the Gospel message: that God, though it may at times appear otherwise, has not forsaken us.

The curation of this anthology is the work of Elizabeth Dias, TIME's religion writer. While people of many faiths have valuable insights into Jesus and his ministry, this collection was drawn from authors who self-identify as Christians. Within that tradition we sought diversity: the collection is ecumenical, uniting writers whose Christian spheres could not be more different. The contributors are Catholics, mainline Protestants, evangelicals and Eastern Orthodox; men, women, LGBT, straight, black, white, Latino and Asian; musicians, painters, essayists, poets, theologians, producers, preachers and nuns. We found them everywhere from Gulu, Uganda, to London's Lambeth Palace to a farm in northeastern Georgia in the American South.

These questions invite the reader to imagine, to question and to participate in stories beyond ourselves. Each author sparks new life into words we've heard countless times.

Often we think of Jesus as a spiritual informer. But his questions show him to be a human inviter. His questions, when gathered together, form their own powerful poem. Humans ask things of the divine all the time, but what did God ask us? Why? What does that mean? Questions about questions can open new frontiers even as we explore the most familiar territories.

Nancy Gibbs *is the editor of* TIME *and a co-author of two best-selling books:* The Presidents Club: Inside the World's Most Exclusive Fraternity *and* The Preacher and the Presidents: Billy Graham in the White House.

ELIZABETH DIAS

INTRODUCTION

Jesus' questions can be easy to miss if you aren't looking for them. It is only when you pause in the forest of his teachings that they appear—like birds camouflaged in the treetops, ready to take flight. And once you spot them, they command your attention, taking you with them as they dart to new branches, sing new melodies and land where you might not expect.

What Did Jesus Ask? is a new collection of these movements and songs as observed by today's best-known disciples, as each pauses to ponder a question Jesus asked in the Gospels. These pages feature storied voices—Ecumenical Patriarch Bartholomew, Sarah Young, Otis Moss III and Marilynne Robinson—and rising ones—Neichelle R. Guidry, founder of shepreaches, a development organization for millennial African-American women in ministry; Carrie Newcomer, a Quaker songwriter; and Archbishop Blase J. Cupich, Pope Francis' appointee in Chicago.

Contributors chose which of Jesus' questions they wanted to consider, and everyone had the same instructions: to reflect on the question itself, not on an answer to it, and to envision the question in a modern way. Beyond that, we left the authors to their own imaginations, and the results are as diverse as the traditions from which the authors come. Cardinal George Pell, who is overhauling the Vatican's financial system, draws on the words of Pope John Paul II. Gene Luen Yang, a graphic artist writing *Superman* for DC Comics, designs a comic strip exploring Jesus' facial expressions. Walter Brueggemann, an Old Testament scholar, writes a poem. Theologian Grace Ji-Sun Kim reflects on her mother's battle with cancer.

This book presents Jesus' questions in their Gospel order—Matthew, Mark, Luke and John—to follow the biblical structure and story. The questions are in the NIV translation for uniformity; a handful of authors mention different versions in their reflections, as noted in parentheses. These include the English Standard Version (ESV), the Revised Standard Version (RSV), the New Revised Standard Version (NRSV) and the New Living Translation (NLT).

Jesus asked more questions than this book contains. The Gospels mention at least 100 others; many are variations or repetitions of the questions selected here, and some are different entirely. Even these are only ones that history has remembered.

But each reminds us just how human Jesus really was. His story has never just hovered in the air or stayed on a page—first it was lived, and then it was lived anew as each generation that followed made it their own. Our authors heard Jesus' questions in today's world. Their musings ask the rest of us to do the same and imagine for ourselves.

Elizabeth Dias *is a correspondent for* TIME *who covers religion and politics. She has a master's in divinity from Princeton Theological Seminary and lectures at universities across the U.S.*

ARCHBISHOP OF CANTERBURY JUSTIN WELBY

"If you love those who love you, what reward will you get?"

(MATTHEW 5:46)

"Oh my soul ... be prepared for him who knows how to ask questions."
—*T.S. Eliot, "Choruses From the Rock"*

It's very often the questions that matter. Answers take us straight to a course of action, but questions shift the responsibility, make us think and leave it up to us.

Jesus was very good at questions. He says, "You've heard that it was said, 'Love your neighbors and hate your enemy,' but I tell you, love your enemies and pray for those who persecute you ... If you love those who love you, what are you doing more than others? Do not the pagans do that?"

Being someone who writes and gives sermons, I understand answers are always the easiest way to go. A good motto for a preacher (which most of us ignore) is "Stand, speak up, shut up." Jesus was brief: to read the whole Sermon on the Mount takes

1

no more than a few minutes, but the questions it poses are life changing.

And that puts me on the back foot. Some of the most important moments of my life have been in response to questions, as they are for most of us. "Will you marry me?," "Will you accept this job?" and most of all from God, "Will you follow me?"

They are the sorts of questions that turn a conversation on a sixpence, and as a silence falls, we find that we have to give an answer.

The question Jesus put forward about loving our enemies is one that few of us can answer easily. It has so many assumptions in it that are uncomfortable for most of us. It assumes that we want our lives to be different from those of other people. It assumes that we will all have enemies of one kind or another. Yet most of us like to blend with the crowd and be at least tolerated, preferably popular, with as many people as possible. But sadly, loving your enemies tends not to win you any friends. It alienates those who think you're going soft and seldom turns your enemies into friends.

Of course, if we're living worthwhile lives we are likely to generate some enemies. I remember once sitting at supper with someone while I was doing some mediation between two warring groups. He said to me, "If you go on doing this, you do realize that someone is likely to try and get at you." I said, "Thank you for the warning. I'm grateful." He looked puzzled.

The warning was repeated twice more, and both times I thanked him, although on each occasion I wondered why he was becoming more and more emphatic. Then my mobile phone buzzed; there was a text from someone who knew us both, saying, "Whatever you do, do not meet with X." X was sitting opposite me. I hadn't realized that he was trying to threaten me rather than merely in a friendly way trying to warn me. Even trying to do the right thing gets us enemies from those who profit from wrong things happening.

There is almost no point in anyone's life that could be more at variance with what happens in the world around us than this: that we should love our enemies. And like all the most important things in Christian discipleship, it starts with the nature of God. St. Paul, in his letter to the Romans, says that God loved us while we were still his enemies, and loved us so much that he made the way for us to become his friends. St. John's Gospel, 3:16, says, "God so loved the world that he gave his only son, so that all who believed in him should not perish but have eternal life."

Enemy is not a category that Jesus Christ uses to decide how he relates to people. That means that we do not have the possibility of adopting that category ourselves to decide on how *we* treat people. His question is more costly than we can imagine. To offer an enemy an open hand instead of a clenched fist carries with it the risk that they will drill a nail into the palm of our hand. They did it to Jesus.

Yet in the world that surrounds us, where making enemies seems so easy, and being someone else's enemy can be something that happens by accident because of our ethnicity, nationality, gender or sexuality, this is the question that each of us needs to answer.

Do we think that love is only for those we find easy to love, or are we willing to love those who hate us?

One of the greatest privileges of my role as Archbishop is to meet people who take Jesus at his word and find a liberation and freedom in committing themselves to love their enemies, a freedom that they never had when they were locked up in hatred. I'm deeply moved whenever I come across it. I find it by mass graves in Africa, in hospitals in Peshawar, Pakistan, and just in people I meet casually.

Everywhere I find it I am struck once again not simply by the frailty and beauty of humanity choosing to love but by the presence of Jesus who makes it possible.

The Most Reverend and Right Honorable Justin Welby *is the Archbishop of Canterbury, the leader of the Church of England.*

"Can any one of you by worrying add a single hour to your life?"

(MATTHEW 6:27)

—•••—

This question might as well be a live worm on a hook, because the minute you answer it you are a goner. You can argue with Jesus all you like—tell him that worrying about your weight gets you to the gym twice a week, or that worrying about your job prospects makes you study harder—but can you say for sure that this will add an hour to your life? No, you cannot, which is why you are hooked—so hooked that you can already guess what is coming next. *Why do you worry then? Why are you so anxious?* That is what Jesus really wants to know, and for some of us it is the question of a lifetime.

When I looked out my kitchen window this morning, I saw my orange tabby crouching at the foot of the bird feeder. A red-tailed hawk circled high overhead with eyes on the same target. But if the cardinals at the feeder were nervous, they did not let it show. They bent their heads to the sunflower seeds like they had all the time in the world, breaking the hulls in their black beaks with perfect self-possession.

That is why I do not think it was fair for Jesus to ask people about their anxiety level and then point to the birds of the air and the lilies of the field as models of trust in divine providence. Do birds of the air have mortgage payments? Do lilies of the field have aging parents who depend on them for long-term care? No, they do not. Only humans have problems like these, which goes a long way toward explaining why we, of all creatures, are the most anxious.

Why do we worry? We worry because we have been given the gift of human consciousness. We worry because we are able to imagine a future we cannot control. We worry because we are afraid of losing what we love.

When I was a full-time pastor, I was often asked to bless a new home. Sometimes it was a newly purchased house in a leafy suburb, and sometimes it was a new apartment in a public housing project. Either way, it was someone's new dwelling on earth, and the people moving into it wanted to ask God's blessing on the place where they would live. So they invited some of their old friends and new neighbors to join them, trusting me to choose the right words to help them warm their new home.

By the time they opened their door to the guests, the new tenants were usually exhausted. Some had spent all day building shelves or hanging curtains. Others had dug out the wedding china, washing each piece by hand to use for a simple meal afterward. When I arrived with a prayer book in one hand and a bunch of flowers in the other, it was easy to see the pride on their faces along with the tiredness. "Welcome to our new home," they said.

Since some of those present had never been to a house blessing before, I explained that Episcopalians are "people of the Book," with an established order of worship for everything from baptizing babies to burying the dead. It was my way of letting them know that I had not chosen the Bible passage I was about to read—the one that is always read at the blessing of a new home—and which can sound like a rebuke to the people who have just worked so hard to get everything right.

> *Therefore I tell you, do not worry about your life, what you will eat or what you will drink, or about your body, what you will wear. Is not life more than food, and the body more than clothing? Look at the birds of the air; they neither sow nor reap nor gather into barns, and yet your heavenly Father feeds them. Are you not of more value than they? And can any of you by worrying add a single hour to your span of life? (Matthew 6:25–27, NRSV)*

If that was ever a comfort to anyone, no one ever mentioned it to me. Instead, we let the words hang in the air while we began our procession, going from room to room lighting fresh candles in each one before asking God's blessing on what would happen there. In the kitchen we asked a blessing on the hands that would work there, along with the gift of grateful hearts for daily bread. In the bedroom we asked a blessing on those who would sleep there, wishing them hours of rest and refreshment. We even had a prayer for the bathroom, where we asked a blessing on those who would care for their bodies there, keeping them "clean and fair, whole and sound."

> *Give us this day our daily bread.*
> *Now I lay me down to sleep.*
> *Cleanse me with hyssop, and I will be clean.*

By the time we returned to the living room, our luminous attention to the rhythms of an ordinary day had taken the edge off Jesus' commandment against worrying. He *was* a bird of the air, after all. He was a lily of the field with no place to lay his head, which may be how he got so wise about the futility of anxiety. If he was truly human, as Christians insist he was, then he worried as much as anyone about losing what he loved. He just figured out how to let the loving surpass the losing.

On days when I am having a hard time following his lead, it is sometimes enough to remember the distinction. However many hours I have to live this life, with however little power to keep from losing even one of them, I do this day love being alive.

Barbara Brown Taylor *is an Episcopal priest, best-selling author and professor of religion at Piedmont College in Georgia.*

ADAM HAMILTON

"Why do you see the speck in your neighbor's eye, but do not notice the log in your own eye?"

(MATTHEW 7:3, NRSV)

—•••—

Near the end of the Sermon on the Mount, Jesus asks his hearers, "Why do you see the speck in your neighbor's eye, but do not notice the log in your own eye? Or how can you say to your neighbor, 'Let me take the speck out of your eye,' while the log is in your own eye?" With just a few words Jesus once again displays his oh-so-irritating habit of exposing the less flattering aspects of the human condition.

Yet like the master preacher he is, Jesus uses one of his favorite rhetorical devices, hyperbole—an exaggeration to the point of absurdity—to disarm his hearers, even to make them smile a bit as they try to picture the image of a log in their eye. It takes a minute before the smile fades and they realize that Jesus has exposed their sin.

Like nearly everything else Jesus says, this brief saying is so penetrating and so universally applicable—2,000 years later a preacher need only read the text, with no further commentary, and people get at least part of the point and they sense that Jesus is telling the truth about them.

What is it in us that leads us to need to point out the flaws of others when we've got so many flaws of our own? Why do we take delight in criticizing others behind their backs? Why do we feel the need to offer unsolicited advice? What leads us to be blind to our own shortcomings? Why do we have 20/20 vision when seeing the shortcomings of others?

It doesn't take a clinical psychologist to observe that often the things we're most critical of in others are the things we dislike in ourselves. I've known people who came to despise others whose bad habits and foibles most closely resembled their own. In other cases those most critical, most anxious to reach for the tweezers to remove the speck in the other's eyes, are those who struggle most with their insecurities. When Jesus asks, "Why do you see the speck in your neighbor's eye?," is it possible that he's doing more than asking us to acknowledge our propensity to judge? Perhaps he really does want us to wrestle with the "why." Maybe he is trying to get us to take a serious look within to see what motivates us to point out the speck in our neighbor's eye.

On a side note, some preachers feel the need to defend the practice of judging, so they seek to clarify what Jesus *really* meant by this pithy little saying. We have to do *some* judging, don't we? And didn't Jesus regularly judge others, calling the religious leaders of his time hypocrites, vipers and whitewashed tombs?

Hmm. Who were those people Jesus was judging again? He showed compassion for the prostitutes, the traitors, the adulterers, the foreigners, the people who were divorced multiple times, the materialists and more. Most often when Jesus judges, he judges religious leaders who are into judging other people!

Of course we have to judge, and this short saying of Jesus' with its two questions actually calls us to judge, but note that the person it calls me to judge is me: "Take the log out of your own eye." Perhaps the most unnerving thing in this saying of Jesus' is not his call for me to stop judging others but this command for me to start judging myself—to take the log(s) out of my own eye!

A strange thing happens to our vision as we get older. We can't see things up close so well anymore. I now have trifocals. My wife wears readers. Without our glasses, we need our friends to hold the menu across the table if we want to have a chance at actually reading it.

I wonder if the same thing happens spiritually, diminishing our capacity to see the things in ourselves that are misaligned with God's will. Maybe this is why it's so easy to see the splinter in someone else's eye. One would think that the older we get, the less judgmental we would be, but sometimes as we get older, we struggle to see our shortcomings while our sensitivity to the feelings of others begins to fade. We find ourselves feeling justified to speak our minds, regardless of the pain we inflict upon others.

The wisest people I know regularly ask others to help them see the logs in their own eyes, while only pointing out the specks in another's eyes when asked. And wise is the person who, when asked to help find the splinter in someone else's eye, does so believing and expressing that they have large logs in their own eyes. Often it is hearing another openly confessing the logs in their own eyes that makes it possible to ask for help.

This leads me back to where we started. Jesus felt compelled to tell his followers not to spend their energy judging others and to assume a humble posture that recognized they had logs in their own eyes. Perhaps he knew how easy it would be for Christians, pastors and churches in the centuries ahead to focus on pointing out the sins of others. Perhaps he knew that by the beginning of the third millennium, young adults would describe the reason they were opting out of church as the judgmentalism they experience from Christians and in churches. I suspect that millennials feel a strong resonance with Jesus' words on judging and logs and specks; they simply seldom see Christians living them. Those churches that ignore Jesus' words about logs and splinters will struggle in the years ahead at reaching today's young adults. But those that practice them stand a chance of reversing the trend among young adults who find Jesus compelling but have been turned off by his followers.

Adam Hamilton *is the senior pastor at the United Methodist Church of the Resurrection in Leawood, Kans., and author of* Making Sense of the Bible.

SARAH YOUNG

"You of little faith, why are you so afraid?"

(MATTHEW 8:26)

—•••—

"You of little faith, why are you so afraid?" This is the question Jesus asked his disciples in the midst of a furious storm—one that came without warning.

Jesus had been teaching crowds of people on the western shore of the Sea of Galilee. He and his disciples were in a boat heading toward the eastern shore, a less populated area.

The Sea of Galilee is nearly 700 ft. below sea level and is surrounded by high mountains that rise thousands of feet into the air. When strong winds sweep into this deep valley, they often give rise to sudden, violent storms. This was one such storm, and it completely unnerved the disciples—even though some of them were very seasoned fishermen.

Jesus wasn't afraid. In fact, he was sound asleep until his disciples woke him, pleading for help: "Lord, save us! We are going to drown!" Jesus called these terrified men "you of little faith." This was his recurring rebuke when his followers weren't trusting in him. However, it was a gentle rebuke, followed by a caring question:

"Why are you so afraid?" Jesus wanted to help his disciples handle their fear—just as he wants to help *us* with our many fears.

After Jesus spoke to his ever-so-human disciples, he rebuked the winds and the waves with superhuman power. Speaking briefly but with sovereign authority, Jesus said, "Peace, be still!" Immediately, the sea became calm. The raging elements of nature, cowed by his command, obeyed instantly.

The disciples were amazed as they witnessed this dramatic demonstration of Jesus' deity. Their friend who had been weary enough to sleep through a raging storm had shown himself powerful enough to quell it supernaturally, with only a few words.

To help calm the storms in *my* life, I wrote the daily devotional book *Jesus Calling: Enjoying Peace in His Presence*. It is written in the voice of Jesus speaking to you, the reader. The following excerpt is based on Jesus' command to the wind and the waves. Perhaps it will speak to the storms in your life.

> *Do not be afraid, for I am with you. Hear Me saying,* "Peace, be still," *to your restless heart. No matter what happens,* I will never leave you or forsake you. *Let this assurance soak into your mind and heart until you overflow with Joy.* Though the earth give way, and the mountains fall into the heart of the sea, *you need not fear!* (Mark 4:39; Deuteronomy 31:6; Psalm 46:2)

When I am feeling anxious or fearful, it's helpful to remember Jesus' soothing yet potent words: "Peace, be still!" Because he is all-powerful and all-knowing, Jesus is fully capable of helping me—and *you*. He is always with us, eager to help us with our fears. His words encourage us to be still in his presence, remembering who he is. Jesus' peace can soothe our troubled hearts.

Shortly after I was asked to write this essay, my then 3-week-old grandson, Caleb, developed such a high fever that he had to be hospitalized. I had already been pondering the question assigned to me: "You of little faith, why are you so afraid?" The crisis with Caleb's health made the question poignantly relevant.

Throughout that difficult time, my daughter Stephanie faced her fears with remarkable grace and peace. From Caleb's hospital room, she wrote the following account of her ordeal:

I have been allowed to face two of my biggest fears these last few days. First was the fear of being physically unable to care for my children, which happened Friday when I woke up with a raging infection. Second was the fear of having my newborn, Caleb, sent to the hospital with a fever—a deep-seated fear after my two-year-old-son, John, had two very close calls in his first month of life. And here I sit in a hospital room with Caleb hooked up to an IV after he spiked a fever Saturday night.

And yet these experiences I have dreaded for so long have been full of God's comforting presence. Yes, it has been painful, emotional, and exhausting. But through it I have had unusual peace, knowing that God is in this. God graciously allowed all of this to happen during the short time when my parents were already here visiting, giving me peace that Elie [Stephanie's daughter] and John are being well cared for despite my inability to do so myself. God gave me peace through the tears as Caleb got poked more than any person deserves, much less a tiny baby. I've had peace through the sleepless nights in the hospital.

And now Caleb is improving so that we should be allowed to go home this afternoon. As I reflect on these difficult days, I see that God can truly conquer my fears.

As I marveled at Stephanie's calm courage, I remembered a

long-ago time when I was a seminary student struggling with academic pressures, the flu and a car accident. This was a furious storm to me. One day I was tearfully relating my troubles to a friend, when her 3-year-old daughter looked into my eyes and asked, "Don't you know that Jesus is taking care of you?" In her sweet, precocious way, she was asking, "You of little faith, why are you so afraid?"

Unable to answer the child's question, I accepted her gentle rebuke and rested in Jesus' presence. Similarly, the disciples in the boat with Jesus were unable to answer his question. Instead, they asked one another, "What kind of man is this? Even the winds and the waves obey him!" I think this was a rhetorical question—an exclamation of amazement and awe, with a newfound reverence in his holy presence.

What the disciples had seen and heard on that unforgettable day was sufficient—sufficient to know that Jesus is Immanuel: *God with us.* Because he is God and he is always with us, we don't need to be afraid.

Sarah Young *is the best-selling author of* Jesus Calling.

JAMES MARTIN, SJ

"Do you believe that I am able to do this?"

(MATTHEW 9:28)

The most difficult question that the modern, rational, intelligent person can ask about the Gospels may be this: How can I believe that these things really happened? This, in essence, is the question that Jesus poses in the Gospel of Matthew to two blind men who ask Jesus, in so many words, to be healed: "Do you believe that I am able to do this?"

Jesus' question comes in the middle of a rapid-fire series of four different healings in Matthew's Gospel. A woman who had been suffering from internal bleeding for 12 years secretly approaches Jesus in a crowd, touches the hem of his garment and is cured of her affliction. Immediately afterward, Jesus enters the house of a synagogue official whose daughter is thought to be dead and says to the crowd, "The girl is not dead, she is only asleep." After the crowd laughs at him, Jesus enters the house and either heals the girl or restores her to life. Then comes the story of the two blind men, and after that, Jesus heals a man who is "possessed by a demon."

It's not surprising that the crowds say, "Never has anything like this been seen in Israel!"

But again the question is: How can I believe these outlandish stories?

Many people see Jesus of Nazareth as a wise prophet, a compassionate teacher and an inspiring leader but stop short of believing him to be divine or possessing any supernatural powers. So they often set aside the miracle stories.

Yet the statement that Jesus acted as a healer and exorcist has as much reliability as almost any other statement that we can make about Jesus of Nazareth. In fact, those stories have *more* corroboration—that is, they are repeated and referred to in a variety of places throughout the Gospels—than do many other statements about Jesus that people often take for granted. Moreover, a great many of Jesus' best-known sayings and teachings, which we also take for granted, are set in the context of healings and exorcisms.

Of course in Judaea and Galilee in the 1st century, physical illnesses were sometimes conflated with demonic possession. When Jesus cures a boy with epilepsy, for instance, different Gospels describe the boy as either suffering from epilepsy (literally in the original Greek: "moonstruck") or being afflicted by a "spirit." The Gospel writers were not modern-day diagnosticians, so it is sometimes unclear if some of the illnesses were psychosomatic in nature.

But many of the illnesses described by the Gospel writers are clearly *not* psychosomatic. Leprosy (which encompassed a variety of skin conditions), blindness, withered limbs and so on cannot be attributed to something that is in one's mind. And whether or not people thought some illnesses were the result of demons, the point is that Jesus heals people from serious and sometimes life-long afflictions—and does so immediately.

In other words, there is a reason the crowds are continually "amazed," as the Gospels say. Even his disciples, no matter how many times they witness a cure, are "astonished." "We have never seen anything like this!" they say after he heals a paralyzed man in Capernaum, a town by the Sea of Galilee.

The fact that Jesus healed people was never a source of contro-versy in his lifetime. Not even his fiercest opponents doubt that he performed miracles. The controversy is over *when* he does them (on the Sabbath, for example, which incurs the wrath of some of the Jewish leadership) and the *source* of his power (as when some of his opponents accuse him of deriving his power from Satan). Again, the healings are an essential part of Jesus' public ministry.

Nonetheless, many people avoid, downplay and even ignore them. Why? They disturb us. Thomas Jefferson went so far as to scissor out all the miracles from the Gospels to create his own story of Jesus. He wanted a Jesus who didn't threaten, a Jesus he could tame. Yet if we cut out the miraculous from his life, it's not Jesus we're talking about any longer. It's our own creation.

The objection that Jesus could not do miracles may come from the same reasoning that says that God does not exist, or if God does exist then God is not all-powerful. Even devout Christians may play down the miracle stories as a way of making Jesus more "credible" for modern-day audiences. For instance, preachers and homilists will often say that the miracle of the multiplication of loaves and fishes, when Jesus fed a vast crowd with just a small amount of food, was not a miracle per se. Rather, what happened that day on the shores of the Sea of Galilee was that the crowds shared what little food they had, and enough was provided for everyone.

Then the preacher will say, "And isn't that just as miraculous as if Jesus had multiplied the loaves and fishes?"

To which I answer no. This easy-to-digest interpretation reflects the unfortunate modern desire to explain away the inexplicable and to downplay miracles in the midst of a story filled with the miraculous. Almost *one-third* of Mark's Gospel, for example, is devoted to Jesus' miracles. To my mind, some of the interpretations that seek to water down the miracle stories reflect unease with God's power and Jesus' divinity, discomfort with the supernatural and, more basically, an inability to believe in God's ability to do anything.

It also is solipsistic. Such rationalizing explanations, which reflect a desire to explain away all that we cannot understand, are often based on a principle that can be summarized as follows: "What does not happen now did not happen then. If no one can cure a blind person now, then Jesus did not heal a blind person either." It also suggests that historical events can and should be interpreted only through earthly cause and effect, with no supernatural explanation. Finally, it suggests that there are no unique historical figures. Such an approach reduces Jesus to the status of everyone else, when he was completely unique.

More basically, as I mentioned, it reflects a discomfort with Jesus' divinity. But to me, the idea that the Creator of the Universe could enable his Son to heal illnesses is rather easy to believe. If you can create the universe from nothing, then healing a paralyzed man seems a relatively simple thing.

When Jesus asked the two blind men, "Do you believe I can do this?" he is implicitly asking us the same question—or questions: Do you believe that I am the Son of God? Do you believe that I have divine power? In short, do you believe that nothing is impossible with God? These are essential questions for anyone encountering Jesus in the Bible.

The blind men answered yes, and then they were able to see. We are invited to do the same.

James Martin, SJ, *is a Jesuit priest and editor at large of* America *and the author of* Jesus: A Pilgrimage.

"What did you go out into the wilderness to see?"

(MATTHEW 11:7)

I'm a fourth-generation Oklahoman, which means my relatives have been there as long as it has been a state.

We got there following a hodgepodge set of routes. One family barely survived the terror of the Trail of Tears. Another arrived in a wagon train, dirt-poor and desperate for free land. Yet another came to set up a drug business in a wild cow town called Oklahoma City. There was also a shady uncle, who, running from the law, saw the land then called Indian Territory as the safest place to hide. I imagine more routes, too, that the family has chosen not to remember—even darker ones.

Despite these different routes, when my family tells each generation of grandkids our stories, an old-style theme pulls them proudly together. Circumstance, we say, threw our people out to the far edge of American cultural norms and dared us to live. We were given wilderness and told to dig a new life out of prairie dirt. Needless to say, at every turn, our fingers and knees bled.

It's never told as a pretty story. It just is what it is.

If Jesus had turned to my great-grandparents and asked them the same question he asked the crowds in ancient Palestine, What did you go out into the wilderness to see?, their answer would have come quickly: What? The wilderness? Well, first off, it's never nice, rarely planned, always harsh and usually violent. Also, it can be so beautiful it stops your breath, and sometimes, some very rare times, it gives things that are miraculously good—that is, when it isn't horrid beyond words.

Oh yes, they would have added, God's out there, with us, too.

I think back to these tales of wilderness when my feelings about Christianity and the church I serve start to feel a little wobbly, especially when I've been listening to a certain kind of conservative Christian pabulum. It bothers me to see the faith of my grandparents turned into a starched-white story of Christians who live in perfect families, own guns, vote Republican and believe that one day they will be rich.

In reality, this picture describes no one I know. And most especially not anyone who has ever been near any kind of wilderness. And who hasn't?

Even Jesus went there. In his time, the meaning wasn't much different from the wilderness my grandparents knew. In the biblical world, *wilderness* referred to a place outside the domesticated, modernized world of the known, a place where human rules and standards didn't apply.

In ancient times it was also believed that monsters dwelled in the wilderness. All sorts of awful, horrible creatures roaming free, without boundaries or constraint. Remember, Jesus meets the devil there. It's no wonder that people believed that no one but outcasts and so-called crazies would voluntarily go there, men like the wild John the Baptist and the crazed revolutionary, Jesus.

To get a general sense of what wilderness represents, just imagine something, anything, that you value and know to be true. Good things. Things that are beautiful to you. Now throw those things across the room and watch them shatter against the wall. Those shards are what wilderness meant to the folks of Jesus' time.

During the everyday, the far-off wilderness is where we shove the uncertain, the unknown. It is the loose floorboard under which we stuff our temptations and hurts, crossing our fingers that they might stay quiet for a while. Sometimes it's been so long since we've been in the wilderness that we can't even remember all that we've squirreled away there.

Knowing this, is it any wonder that the wilderness is Jesus' first stop?

I think Jesus knew what we all—deep down, behind our navels—know, that until he faced his floorboard, he could not be the leader he needed to be. He knew that he had to honestly amble with his desire for power and spectacle in the barren desert and that avoiding the wilderness would not make it go away.

"What did you go out into the wilderness to see?" he asks—perhaps with a pregnant smile—knowing that in the wilderness, nothing less than the truth awaits.

John the Baptist roams the wilderness and returns with a prophetic message against the state and religious elites who ultimately kill him. The wilderness never leaves John, even with a rising temptation to capitulate and become like the earthly powerful.

The constant facade of order hides the wilderness that is

craving to seep out and teach us that life wasn't created to be what we think it is. Beyond words, we must experience the wilderness to be taught what cannot be otherwise known.

While order may tempt us to rely on growth and production and marginal revenue to secure happiness, we must remember that the very existence of wilderness depends on shutting down the systems and structures that are destroying our climate. In the wilderness, we see the abundance of creation without the strain of capitalist structures.

We must also venture into the wilderness of human relationships—a place where so much is spoken, yet more is unspoken. Once there, even a quick look around reveals the structural inequalities that exist in human interaction. The wilderness reveals that the communities we create are not blind to race, creed, gender or sexual orientation.

When returning from the wilderness to the order of religious and urban life, I am tempted to think that keeping this wilderness with me means simply to call out the evils that were so clearly revealed. Yet I am exposed to the limitations of my own capacity for and the intricate complexity of shaping a theologically and socially conscious response to evil. The wilderness does not give us clear answers, but it beckons us to proclaim what it has shown us.

My family went to Oklahoma and found God there. We must follow deeper into the great prophetic tradition of wilderness and, once there, not be afraid when we can't make sense of it all. That which it shows us must guide our steps as we reinvigorate a world of false order with the mystery of wilderness.

Serene Jones *is the president of Union Theological Seminary.*

"If any of you has a sheep and it falls into a pit on the Sabbath, will you not take hold of it and lift it out?"

(MATTHEW 12:11)

···

Jesus invites us to actively participate in the work of mercy and compassion toward our neighbors, and these works of mercy and compassion cannot be limited by our obligations of time.

This parable tells a story of a sheep that fell into a pit on a day the Israelites were forbidden to work. The shepherd whom Jesus spoke of in this passage clearly ignored the law to save his sheep.

While the action of the shepherd may seem reasonable to us today, and possibly to the people who first heard this parable some 2,000 years ago, the truth is, there was no shortage—then or now—of religious leaders who would rather abide by the letter of the law than become vulnerable by showing mercy to someone in great need.

I believe that an active participation in reaching out to those who have fallen into the pit of vulnerability, poverty, ignorance or disease is deeply rooted in our relationship with God. Many of us know the greatest commandments of loving God with our heart, soul and mind, and of loving our neighbors as we love ourselves, but this parable teaches us something in addition: that there is no boundary of time when it comes to liberating others from bondage, injustice and destruction.

For more than a decade in northern Uganda, tens of thousands of young women and children were dispossessed by terrorists who called themselves the Lord's Resistance Army. Kidnapped and forced to commit atrocities against their own families and neighbors, these victims were trained to be killers as child soldiers, with the girls then being forced into sex slavery.

And yet, over the past 20 years, I have witnessed many of these girls and their babies being pulled out of that traumatic pit through love and compassion. This work has been done through the loving service of the Sisters of the Sacred Heart of Jesus Christ, of which I am one. While many politicians and legalistic religious leaders looked away, we accepted these young women and children, many of whom were unable to hide visible scars on their faces and bodies as well as socially unacceptable stigmas such as being pregnant and unmarried and/or HIV-positive.

While so many caregivers, charitable institutions and religious organizations chose to flee the violence and chaos of northern Uganda and southern Sudan, my sisters and I had no choice but to run directly toward the center of the conflict, for that was where the most vulnerable were. Even to this day, I recall places that seemed "the bottom of the bottom, the worst of the worst."

Obviously, we were frightened and shocked by the overwhelming sense of evil that continued to surround us and the young women and children we were called to serve. But in moments such as those, we relied on the fact that God remained present with us, and we were simply doing what Italian Comboni Missionaries and African nuns did for many of us when we were forced to deal with violence and civil war as children, and for many of the sisters, as orphans of war.

I made the decision that the best way to save the children abducted by Joseph Kony of the Lord's Resistance Army was to speak to them over the radio airwaves, giving them clear directions on where they could find refuge for themselves and their children. This approach meant that the terrorists listening to the radio could find us as well, but we took the risk anyway.

Once the girls were able to find us, they were given a home to live in, unconditional love for their healing and vocational and educational training for themselves and their children. It was, and remains to this day, the mission at St. Monica's Girls' Tailoring Centre, where these girls are taught how to love again, how to forgive the wrongs done to them and how to look to the future with hope. This doesn't happen overnight. For some, it may take the rest of their lives.

Like the shepherd in the parable, we often went against the grain of religious teachers and leaders who were afraid to get their hands or robes dirty or become affiliated with young women known to commit heinous crimes. I still do, to this day. Not out of disrespect to pious men and women of faith, but by following in the example of our Lord, Jesus Christ. Somehow, so many people of faith even today have forgotten that the Son of God surrounded himself with the worst of the worst sinners of his time.

How is it that so many Christians are scared or afraid to do the same?

Whether we are in northern Uganda, South Sudan or somewhere in the middle of America, we often allow rules and regulations to limit the time we allocate for genuine acts of mercy and compassion, ignoring the fact that the Sabbath was made for us and that we are created to be God's hands.

I strongly believe our prayer life and spirituality is determined by our acts of compassion to our brothers and sisters in need. Today these precious words of Jesus invite humanity to actively participate in the work of mercy and compassion wherever we may be, whoever we are and no matter what we're doing right now.

For all of my friends of faith, whether they be Catholic or Protestant, Jewish or Muslim, and for all of my friends who don't believe in or understand the concept of a loving God, do we not owe it to one another to leave our world better than the one we were given?

Sister Rosemary Nyirumbe *is a Roman Catholic nun and the director of St. Monica's Girls' Tailoring Centre in Gulu, Uganda.*

"Who is my mother, and who are my brothers?"

(MATTHEW 12:48)

—•••—

Once after Mass, a youngster asked me, "Why do you call us brothers and sisters? You're not my brother." Reasoning that he already had a family, my young interlocutor wondered how we could be brothers. I responded, "Ah, but I am spiritually your brother because we are all members of God's family." After the boy received a nod from his parents, he said approvingly, "Wow, I didn't know that."

In the Gospel, we hear Jesus ask, "Who is my mother? Who are my brothers?"

This had to have been confusing to his listeners. After all, his family was standing right outside. So what did he mean?

When Jesus next answers his own questions—"Whoever does the will of my heavenly Father is my brother, and sister, and mother"—we can see he is teaching us to broaden our horizons, to think beyond the idea of natural family. At the same time, he is inviting us to be part of his own family—one big family of God.

Jesus' disciples throughout history—the church—have listened to his words and understood that he means more than a metaphor or a poetic figure of speech. In asking these questions and giving this answer about being his family, Jesus shows us that he came to do more than teach us a philosophy. Above all else, he wants a personal relationship with us. He wants to share his life with us. In addition to the families we grow up in, as that youngster at Mass discovered, the Lord asks us to be part of a real spiritual family in communion with him by doing the will of God.

So the real questions we must ask ourselves are: What is the will of Christ's heavenly Father so that we too might be his family? More personally, what is God's will for *us*? What does it mean for *you* and for *me* to be Jesus' mother, brother, sister?

Throughout his ministry, Jesus said he came to do the will of the Father who sent him (e.g., John 6:38). He ministered to the sick, brought glad tidings to the poor and proclaimed liberty to captives. In the Sermon on the Mount, the Lord told of the new way of life. It involves the merciful, those who hunger and thirst for righteousness, those who mourn, the peacemakers and the poor in spirit. Later in his ministry, his disciples are challenged to envision a world in which the hungry are fed, the thirsty are given drink, the stranger is welcomed and the naked are clothed. He says to forgive one another and be a light of goodness to the world. Finally, Jesus gave up his life on the Cross and rose again on the third day to save us from sin and gain eternal life.

In his words and in his deeds, the Lord reveals that he is love personified and that his will is simply that we love him and love one another. "As I have loved you, so you also should love one another" (John 13:34). Loving one another, giving of ourselves, taking the other into our hearts—this is what it means to be family. This is what it means to be Jesus' mother, brother, sister.

To more fully understand Jesus' questions—"Who is my mother? Who are my brothers?"—we need to remember that he is not just any man; he is the Lord. The life he wants to share with us as part of God's family is a divine, eternal life. Having broken the chains of death, he invites us to share in his Resurrection.

Jesus, the Son of God, asks us to call God "Father" as well. As he did with Nicodemus, he invites us to be born again, this time of the Spirit (John 3:1–21). A new life in God's family begins particularly in the waters of baptism as the limits of the old order begin to pass away. "See what love the Father has given us, that we should become children of God and so we are" (1 John 3:1).

As children of God, necessarily we are all then the new spiritual brothers and sisters of Jesus, one family united in love. Is this not the meaning of what Jesus asks with his questions—to be a people who bear fruit through our love, as a mother does, to care and respect one another and to reach out to embrace one another with all the affection of brothers and sisters? Is this not in a very real and profound sense exactly what this world needs today? Would we not all be blessed if, through our love, we were to transform our society into a culture of compassion, understanding, mutual respect and solidarity?

As we journey through life, encountering Jesus along the way, he engages us in dialogue. Here, we can easily envision his questions "Who is my mother? Who are my brothers?" to be a request for a show of hands. Jesus asks us—you and me—"Will you be my mother, my brother, my sister?" He asks us, as he did with Peter, "Do you love me?" (John 21:15). How do we respond?

Cardinal Donald Wuerl *is the Roman Catholic Archbishop of Washington.*

NADIA BOLZ-WEBER

"Why did
you doubt?"

(MATTHEW 14:31)

I've often heard the story of Peter walking on the water preached as a Little Engine That (Almost) Could story. Peter and the disciples are in a boat far from shore when, in the midst of a violent storm, they see Jesus walking toward them on the water. Peter thinks, Walking on water? Cool. Maybe I could do that! And then he does the totally crazy thing of trying. Amazingly, he does it—he actually walks on water for a few steps. You can just hear him, can't you? "I think I can, I think I can." There he is, a soaring monument to high self-esteem and a can-do attitude. He musters up what it takes to be God-like, and what it takes is faith.

If you have enough faith (I have been told in countless sermons on this text), you can do it too—and maybe even better than Peter! With enough faith you can walk on water all the way to Jesus! Preachers then often go on to inform us that Peter's only mistake was that he stopped believing in himself ... I mean, he stopped believing in Jesus. Jesus reaches out to Peter as Peter sinks in the water and says, "Why did you doubt?" I've always heard that question as, "You can do such great, God-like things, Peter—you just have to have enough faith!" Which would mean that the moral of the story (and of course, every Bible story is about how to be moral—so the *how to be moral* of this particular story) is that if you are not yet God-like in your ability to walk on water or financially prosper or overcome your failings as a human, then the problem is that you don't have enough faith. The solution is for you to muster up more faith, because it's up to you to make your way to Jesus. So do not doubt, do not be like Peter, who didn't have enough faith (in himself? In Jesus? It's unclear), but just "I think I can, I think I can" all the way to Jesus. End of sermon.

I guess I don't see that way of telling the story to be good news. I know that for me, "I think I can, I think I can" doesn't seem to make storms less terrifying. So having some preacher tell me that if I just had more faith, I could do the impossible has never helped me navigate my life when I'm being battered by the wind.

I started to think that when Jesus said to Peter, "You of little faith, why did you doubt?," maybe he wasn't referring to the inevitable fact that Peter sank when he stepped out of the boat. Perhaps Jesus' asking Peter why he doubted had less to do with his temporary ability to walk on water than with his temporary inability to believe it was Jesus right there in the middle of a terrifying gale to begin with.

Stormy waters in Scripture are the very image of chaos, the unknown—that turmoil and darkness that must be kept at bay. So when the disciples were caught in a tempest, they thought it more likely that the figure walking toward them was a ghost than the Son of God, since God couldn't possibly be present in such difficulty and fear and uncertainty and instability and chaos. Even after Jesus spoke to them, saying, "It is I, do not be afraid," Peter still doubted. So perhaps Jesus' question to Peter, "Why did you doubt?," pertained less to Peter's doubting he could pull off some mad skills and more to Peter's doubting that God could be present as he struggled with the darkness and chaos of the human experience.

That's why the disciples didn't recognize Jesus walking on the water. Chaos is no place for God. And when we are close to God, so to speak, then things in life should be calm and peaceful and not at all sea-monster-like. If being close to God looked like an apartment, it would be a clean, harmonic, feng shui loft and not a crazy, discordant, dumpster-dive squat. So when life looks more like a squat than a loft, we wonder where God went and how we, in his absence, are going to try and "I think I can, I think I can" our way back to God.

But Jesus disrupts that kind of thinking both for us and the first disciples. It's hard to maintain the idea that the nearness of God is concomitant with a suffering-free life when that same God became human and was present before those who followed him in storms, conflict and betrayal. Jesus didn't stay in some protected, serene, holy building where they could "I think I can" their way to him. Instead he was there walking with them to the store and walking toward them in the storm. He walked through the mundane and the transcendent, the blissful and the terrifying. Jesus was near to human suffering and celebration, messing with everyone's ideas of what having God close by looked like.

Maybe the point for us is not that we can make our way to God if we just listen to our internal power-of-positive-thinking voice— if we muster up enough "faith." Maybe the point is that God is in the chaos with us to begin with. Right there in the muck of things, regardless of whether that is what we think being close to God looks like. Why do you doubt that?

Nadia Bolz-Weber *is the founding pastor of House for All Sinners and Saints in Denver. She is the author of* Accidental Saints: Finding God in All the Wrong People.

LAUREN WINNER

"Why do you break the command of God for the sake of your tradition?"

(MATTHEW 15:3)

—•••—

I have a hunch about why this particular exchange between Jesus and the Pharisees is omitted from the lectionary, the table that spells out which bits of Scripture are proclaimed (and preached on) in church on Sunday mornings: it would be a curiosity to hear the priest read Jesus condemning the ritual washing of hands before eating bread—and then see the priest turn around 15 minutes later and ritually wash her hands before consecrating and eating bread. It would be a curiosity to hear the text and then see the priest undo it—a generative curiosity, one I wish the church had seen fit to provoke.

Christian ways of meeting God are deeply ritualistic—which is another way of saying they are a lot like the Pharisees' ways of meeting God. The Gospel of Matthew, which overflows with harsh criticisms of the Pharisees, doesn't precisely spell out that during Jesus' lifetime, Jewish spirituality was centered on the temple. The temple was understood to be God's nearest dwelling place on earth, and 1st century Jews were accustomed to thinking that they had access to God primarily, or perhaps even exclusively, in the temple and through the temple rites. If you wanted to get close to holy things, if you wanted to get close to God, you went to the temple—and indeed many Jews did just that, making pilgrimages during the holidays of Passover, Sukkot and Shavuot.

As scholar of Judaism Jacob Neusner has argued, the Pharisees aimed to take some of the holiness that was centered in the temple and spread it abroad. This was the Pharisees' project—offering holiness, beyond the temple gates, to ordinary Jewish men and women, in the midst of their ordinary lives. This is why the Pharisees articulated an intricate and demanding choreography of religious observance: to require, say, rigorous Sabbath practice and the wearing of ritual garments was in fact to democratize access to God; the rituals gave people ways to connect their lives to God when they were far from the temple.

And so the Pharisees expected men and women to ritually wash their hands before they ate. Why? Because (to again follow Neusner) the priests did that very thing before offering a sacrifice in the temple, and the Pharisees sought to turn every household, every home, into a temple—not for the sake of punctiliousness but for the sake of holiness. Your own dinner table can be a place of divine encounter—so just as the priest makes himself ritually pure before approaching the altar, you should do likewise before sitting down to lunch.

Jesus' question about God's commandments and tradition, Jesus' seeming disdain for ritual hand-washing before the meal, is part of a larger, and smaller, fight Jesus had with the Pharisees. It was a fight about tactics but not about goals. At a deep level, the

Pharisees' vision for life with God and Jesus' vision for life with God was the same: both wanted to give more people more access to God. They wanted to offer ordinary men and women intimacy with the God of Israel. They wanted to take the holiness that had been housed primarily in the temple and offer it profligately in people's daily lives.

And so they fought—and fights are often most bitter between those people who are after the same thing but have different ways of going about it. Consider the sustained disagreement, in the 1950s and '60s, between Thurgood Marshall and Martin Luther King Jr. over the best way to pursue the extension of civil rights to African Americans: either through the court system, as Marshall and the NAACP Legal Defense Fund thought, or through nonviolent direct action. The goal was the same, but the means diverged. The divergences were crucial and sometimes spawned bitter invective.

Jesus and the Pharisees differed on tactics. If the Pharisees' tactic was giving people rituals, we might say, simply, that Jesus democratized access to the Lord by actually being the Lord and making himself available to everybody. That tactic is the center-piece of Christian life with God. But Christians surround that centerpiece with gesture after gesture that is aptly pharisaical.

For years, I did this very thing, this ritual hand-washing, before I abandoned Judaism and became an Episcopalian. Now I do it only as a priest, before handling the about-to-be body of Jesus, bread made thus by God, God making it thus with my ritu-ally washed hands.

Before other meals, regular meals at my table at home or at a restaurant, I make other ritual gestures with my hands. I hold hands for prayer, if I am not eating alone; I cross my body, sometimes, with the fingers of my hand. These gestures, like the gesture of ritually dousing one's hands with water, are just ways of placing my body, and my feeding of that body, before the Lord.

Eating, walking, having sex, sleeping; there are always two ways of doing each of these things. One can do them insensibly, almost automatically, or one can do them with intention. To speak, as a Christian, of "intention" is to speak not only of awareness or mindfulness. The intention is to make the thing—the eating, the walking—into an offering to the Lord. There are lots of ways to make something an offering, though since we are bodily creatures, most of the things we do to make something into an offering are pointedly bodily things. So we hold hands, we cross ourselves, we say a prayer, we keep silence. These things, like ritual ablution, can make our eating an act of love, an offering. Jesus' question opposes tradition to commandment. I'd prefer to say that commandments are always handed to us, and that receiving them with washed hands shows our love for them.

Lauren Winner *is an assistant professor of Christian spirituality at Duke Divinity School. Her books include* Girl Meets God, Still: Notes on a Mid-Faith Crisis *and most recently* Wearing God.

JONATHAN L. WALTON

"What good will it be for someone to gain the whole world, yet forfeit their soul?"

(MATTHEW 16:26)

—•••—

Recently I discovered 17th century French playwright Molière's *The Bourgeois Gentleman.* The play mocks the aspirations of those who seek to distinguish themselves from the masses with pretensions of nobility and ostentatious affectations of cultural superiority. It is an incredible lampoon of those obsessed with social status. The play's protagonist, Monsieur Jourdain, pays top dollar for clothes that make him look amusing and awkward. He employs music teachers, a fencing instructor and a philosophy professor for others to see rather than for his desire to learn. And he refuses to let his daughter marry an upstanding middle-class man whom she loves because he prefers any breathing body deemed a nobleman. Monsieur Jourdain wants to be somebody. He wants others to deem him important. Yet the more he seeks the assumed behavioral and material markings of nobility, the more he offends those who really love him and allows himself to look ludicrous to those he seeks to impress.

In contemporary parlance, Monsieur Jourdain might be accused of being a faker or a wannabe. Others might accuse him of conspicuous consumption and crass materialism—infected with what Australian scholars Clive Hamilton and Richard Denniss refer to as the socially contagious disease of "affluenza," symptoms of which include extreme debt, anxiety and waste. But whatever we think of Monsieur Jourdain, none of us should consider him uncommon.

It is safe to say that anxiety about social status is a perennial problem, whether in the 21st century U.S., 17th century France or 1st century Palestine. The Gospel of Matthew presents to us a Jesus who paints an otherworldly picture of the Kingdom of God that inverts traditional social orders of this world. Individuals considered "unclean"—like the woman with the hemorrhage of blood in the Gospel narrative who is healed by Jesus—are redeemed, while self-righteous leaders will be judged (9:20). Those with places of prominence will be displaced, as the uninvited are seated at the center of God's welcome table (22:1). And the first shall be last, and the last first (20:16). In other words, Jesus' Gospel message of grand reversal was one of encouragement and empowerment for the otherwise disenfranchised and disaffected. Thus his message posed a threat to those who put their trust in armies, political power, ecclesial hierarchy and other common markers of social status.

Many credible psychotherapists suggest that our obsession with material goods and acquiring marks of cultural distinction points to our fear and anxiety about the future. This cuts across economic divides. Some people are anxious about having food on the table or enough money to purchase a month's worth of medication. This is understandable. Yet there are also those in our society who are anxious about earning a salary in the mere high six figures when there are others in their social circles who earn millions. Canadian writer Chrystia Freeland documents in her book *Plutocrats: The Rise of the New Global Super Rich and Fall of Everyone Else* that the anxiety created among the bottom of the top 1% vs. the top of the top 0.01% reveals there is something deeper driving our angst than mere economic security. There is a longing for more—a spiritual hunger that neither the delay of death nor being valorized in life can fulfill. As Zora Neale Hurston writes in the first line of *Their Eyes Were Watching God*, "Ships at a distance have every man's wish on board."

This is why Jesus posed this question to his disciples: "What good will it be for someone to gain the whole world, yet forfeit their soul?" It takes courage to ask of ourselves the same question today. What does it profit us to seek and hoard all the things that promise to bring joy yet after the initial contact high tend to leave us with a hangover? Scientific data support what many of us have experienced. Once we reach a certain level of economic stability, there is no correlation between money and happiness. In fact, an international team of researchers from the World Health Organization revealed that those who live in wealthier nations such as France, New Zealand and the U.S. are more likely to suffer from depression and stress than those living in less affluent countries. Like Leo Tolstoy's protagonist in the short story "How Much Land Does a Man Need?," some of us forfeit happiness, if not our very lives, in our incessant pursuit of more. What does it profit us?

On the other hand, several studies have confirmed the link between serving others and overall well-being. Researchers at the University of Exeter Medical School reviewed data from the previous two decades to discover that there is a direct link between volunteerism and lessening symptoms of depression and even risks of dying. Jesus' question pushes us in this direction: Do we want to earn a living, or do we want to earn a life that is worth living? If we accept Jesus' challenge in Matthew 25 to feed the hungry, provide clothes to the naked and visit the imprisoned, maybe we will cease committing soul suicide by seeking false security; we will cease placing our dependence on depreciating assets that ultimately diminish our humanity. Thus investing in human life is not simply about helping those living in the shadows of our society. According to Jesus, in their humanity we find him. In their humanity, we find ourselves. For in God's Kingdom, human life is an asset that never depreciates.

Jonathan L. Walton *is a professor of religion and society at Harvard Divinity School and the minister of the Memorial Church.*

MICHAEL W. SMITH

"If a man owns a hundred
sheep, and one of them
wanders away, will he not
leave the ninety-nine on the
hills and go to look for the
one that wandered off?"

(MATTHEW 18:12)

This is one of my favorite questions that Christ asks us. It is a mysterious question that has a sort of paradox within it. If you're anything like me, it makes you scratch your head!

I'm a songwriter, not a theologian, but here's my take. What grabs my attention is *to whom* he directed this question: his disciples.

It was in response to a question they had asked of him moments before. Always trying to get the inside scoop on the "important stuff," they asked Jesus, "Who is the greatest in the kingdom of heaven?"

I'm sure they were expecting something like "Yeah, guys, sure. I've got this guy lined up named Paul, he's going to be *such* a big shot. Make sure you watch out for this guy, a *major* player in the Kingdom. Yeah, and I'm trying to line up a new King who's going to overthrow the Romans too."

But Jesus does what he always does: he disappoints our appetite for power and intrigue.

He reaches for a child.

He said, "Unless you change and become like children, you will never enter the kingdom."

That was his secret? That was his plan for world domination?

We must become like children. Humble, open, obedient, joyful, risk-taking children.

He then goes on to reprimand and warn the disciples against overlooking the "weak" and the simple.

And that brings us to his final point. A question: "If a man owns a hundred sheep, and one of them wanders away, will he not leave the ninety-nine on the hills and go to look for the one that wandered off?"

This question says a lot of things to us, too many for me to enumerate here, but the one that strikes me to the core is the reckless inefficiency of the shepherd's response.

I mean, why not just cut your losses and keep the ninety-nine? What kind of shepherd would put the whole flock at risk to go after just one weak, misguided sheep?

Isn't he supposed to be the *great* shepherd? The *good shepherd?*

I can't support the logic of such a decision. But I can stand behind the results.

See, I was the one.

I was the sheep who lost my way.

And I am so grateful that God was "reckless" enough to come find me.

"Amazing grace, how sweet the sound. I once was lost, but now am found ..."

What kind of shepherd would leave the ninety-nine?

The same shepherd who would reach for a child when asked a question about greatness in the Kingdom. *This* kind of shepherd ... a God who would descend from the heights and perfection of heaven, become a man and die on a cross for hopeless sinners ... lost sheep.

This is the God who made more space in the universe than we could ever use. A "more-than-enough God." A God so extravagant in his love that he leaves the majority to reach the minority.

So how do we respond to this question?

Like I said, I'm no theologian, but I am a husband, a father, a human.

And as I travel this planet, I see a world that is confused and hurting.

I see the one sheep. I see them everywhere. What can we do to go find them? To love them?

I think this is a question Jesus is asking the world. Will we lay down our ideas of self-importance and efficiency and do one act of extravagant love today? Tomorrow? The next day?

He did it for us.

I can't speak for you, but I know how I hope to answer his question.

Michael W. Smith *is a Grammy Award– and Dove Award–winning recording artist and philanthropist who supports the teen club Rocketown, Compassion International and Samaritan's Purse.*

ARCHBISHOP CHARLES CHAPUT

"Haven't you read that at the beginning the Creator 'made them male and female'?"

(MATTHEW 19:4)

—···—

This question grounds one of the Gospel's most disputed teachings of our time: the nature of marriage. Critics today tend to frame our inherited understanding of marriage, so deeply informed by millennia of experience as well as by Scripture, as culturally conditioned or outdated or even bigoted. But Jesus' words to the Pharisees are remarkably obvious and mundane.

"Have you not read that from the beginning the Creator made them male and female ..." Even if we deny the existence of a Creator, we can hardly deny that human beings are by nature gendered creatures.

"... [A] man shall leave his father and mother and be joined to his wife, and the two shall become one flesh." Even if we deny a higher meaning to marital relationships, we can hardly deny that from the very beginning men and women have paired off, that these pairings have included sexual intimacy, that from this unique intimacy children have been born and that those children have gone on to do the same.

These Gospel verses describe simple facts on the ground. There are men, and there are women. They form intergenerational families. This is the way it's always been and always will be.

And the most meaningful words in these verses may be the most unassuming: "For this reason ..." With these words, Jesus, quoting Genesis, connects the fact of humanity's gendered nature with the fact of family formation. Marriage exists, and it is what it is because humans are male and female.

To put it another way: marriage is not an artifact of government or even of culture. It's a function of human nature itself. We're made for marriage. Obviously, that doesn't mean every person is called to the married state. Nor does it guarantee the success of any marriage without a great deal of self-sacrifice and effort on the parts of both husband and wife. It does mean that we're designed as the type of creatures for whom marriage is the most suitable relationship for procreation—that is, a unique participation in co-creating new life with God.

In a different reality, humanity might have had several genders, or one. In a different reality, each nature might be suited to a different type of family structure. But in this reality, we are who we are. In this reality, we're male and female, designed to marry. Why?

In Catholic thought, the love between a husband and a wife takes part in God's own love that Jesus Christ pours out for his church. Married love—when lived as it should be—is totally self-giving. That's the cornerstone of every healthy marriage.

The spouses hold nothing back from one another, including their bodies. Married love is designed to be fruitful. Just as God created us in love, we conceive our children in love. Married love is also oriented toward hope. In being open to new life, it drives out loneliness and affirms the future. And because marriage affirms the future, it can become an engine of hope in a world prone to despair.

But as with the natural world, the ecology of the human spirit is fragile. We too often try to evade or overcome the design of our own nature. The modern heart instinctively resents the idea of obligations and limits. So couples too often hold back from a genuinely unselfish love on the assumption that we each know best what to give away and what to keep for ourselves. And what we hang on to most jealously is usually that aspect of ourselves most oriented toward others: our fertility.

A culture that tends to see pregnancy as a kind of inconvenience or infection denies a key part of our human nature. It closes off the future. It fixes on itself to the exclusion of others. It is, quite literally, unnatural because it's unfruitful.

God doesn't stop loving people when they fall or fail, or don't fit a model of perfection, or their health precludes children, or when the circumstances of their lives wound their ability to persevere in a troubled relationship. But individual challenges don't change the essence of what marriage is or the best path to living it fully and joyfully.

These challenges do highlight two facts. First, our nation talks a good line about the value of marriage and family, but our economy and laws ensure the opposite. We've created a culture that runs on acquisitiveness and impermanence—thin soil for institutions rooted in self-giving. And second, too many Christians do a bad job of living what they claim to believe about marriage, family and a great deal else basic to their faith. In the early church, Christian families and local churches offered an intimate network of support for those among them who were suffering or abandoned. Until we get back to providing that same intimate care for the wounded persons among us, the Christian witness of family life will be compromised.

Nonetheless, what Pope Paul VI described as "the natural family"—mother, father and child, woven together in permanent commitment—remains the most important living cell of society. Marriage is its foundation and guarantee. Families are the first communities of society; they're intimate webs of rights and responsibilities that give members their most grounded identities. When real marriages and families fail to form, persons have no insulation against larger social forces, most notably the state and the market. The biggest deceit of modern culture is the idea of the autonomous individual. No such creature exists. We're interdependent. We need each other. We're made for one another and for God. We're made for enduring and fruitful love.

Jesus' words to the Pharisees are about marriage, but they're also about human nature, happiness and our relationship to a God who loves us so much that he created us in a manner particularly suited to participating in his own creative life. This is because marriage itself cannot be separated from our nature, our happiness and our God. And when we try to separate it, whether in our own lives or in public policy, we damage the human ecology we all share.

Charles Chaput *is the Roman Catholic Archbishop of Philadelphia and served as the official host for Pope Francis' 2015 World Meeting of Families. A Capuchin Franciscan friar, he is the founder of the St. John Vianney Theological Seminary in Denver and a co-founder of the National Catholic Association of Latino Leaders.*

"Why do you ask me about what is good?"

(MATTHEW 19:17)

––•••––

During a visit to a high-security section of an Australian jail, I was surprised to see a small group of prisoners, including at least one murderer, gathered respectfully and affectionately around an elderly nun, one of the jail chaplains.

I mentioned my surprise to an experienced priest chaplain, who explained the prisoners' affection not so much by the presence of the feminine in an all-male environment but by their recognition of her kindness and goodness.

Jesus was hated, but only by a few who engineered his execution. The poor, the sick, those who acknowledged their sins flocked to him, attracted by his miracles but much more by the fact that they judged him to be good. They wanted to hear what he had to say.

The rich young man was a genuine seeker who came to Jesus with a question, not a request. "Teacher, what good thing must I do to get eternal life?"

He was certainly reverent, if overenthusiastic, as he genuflected and described Jesus as good, a term the Jews usually reserved for God himself.

The rich young man's question is important, but it can be asked only by someone who already believes God is good and just. If God is capricious or cruel, the issue of personal merit or demerit is irrelevant.

For these reasons it is not surprising that Pope John Paul the Great used this story—in his finest encyclical, *Veritatis splendor* (1993), the first such papal teaching on foundational morality—as the framework for his initial chapter on freedom and law.

Every major paper in the Western world editorialized on this traditional and fiercely controversial reassertion of Christian teaching called "The Splendor of the Truth." For John Paul, doing good requires knowing the truth, sincerity and accuracy, about human life. This presupposes a genuine human freedom, and more controversially for contemporary sensibilities, John Paul followed St. Augustine in insisting that the rich young man's questing and unease came from God and led to Absolute Goodness, God himself.

This encounter with Jesus is narrated in all three synoptic Gospels (Matthew 19:16, Mark 10:18, Luke 18:19) and reveals the young ruler as an observant Jew who spoke from a shared belief in the one true God.

Therefore his question is not a typical first question for rich young professionals today in our secularized Western world, who have come to realize that what they are doing, the possessions they have, are not enough.

They don't begin their search for meaning by identifying the prerequisites for eternal life, although nearly everyone wonders whether there is life after death. They often clear the ground by rejecting any conspicuous evil in their own lives. Most realize that selfishness does not bring happiness and start to search for ways in which they can contribute, through embracing a cause, or opposing evil, or diminishing suffering and disease, helping the poor to improve their lot.

The acceptance or rejection of monotheism creates two worlds of thought and religion. Within the monotheist tradition, acceptance or rejection of the divinity of Christ, our brother and son of Mary, creates equally important divisions.

Our answers to both these options condition our verdict on Jesus' explanation of the good life, of human flourishing.

Goodness belongs first of all to God. So how do we, like his questioner, regard Jesus' reply that if we want to enter into the good life, we must keep the Jewish commandments? Does Jesus have a special or unique capacity to express the Divine Will?

For many today, Jesus is disconcertingly specific in his prescriptions. No scope is given for individual definitions of the good and the bad. Jesus does not allow us to paint reality in the moral colors we choose. He does not recommend that we dodge the issues by appealing to the primacy of conscience. We might develop and explain his teaching, not distort it, by explaining that goodwill is essential and that people of goodwill are called to recognize moral truths, just as we recognize the truths of health and hygiene. Some situations and activities are life-giving while others are damaging.

There is no longer consensus in the Western world on the foundations of moral thinking, but most today have no problem with, for example, recommending respect for parents and exhortations to brotherly love or with condemnations of murder and perjury.

Condemning adultery is another issue altogether, as Mark and Luke list it as the first of the commandments, while Matthew places it second. Unlike the revolutionary currents in continental Europe, such as communism and Nazism, most of the English-speaking world continues to embrace in a haphazard way many particular Christian moral teachings, but not on issues of sexuality, marriage, family and human life and not on wealth.

After the young ruler had explained truthfully that he already accepted and followed the commandments, Jesus invited him to sell his possessions and give the money to the poor. This was as surprising for him as it is for us. He did not rise to the challenge.

Jesus' contemporaries believed prosperity was a sign of God's blessing, so even his disciples were amazed to hear that it is easier for a camel to go through the eye of a needle than for a rich man to enter God's Kingdom. "Who can be saved?" they asked. It is a question for us too, especially as many of us live more comfortably than most people in human history.

Christ was quite clear that we have to choose between God and money. One or the other must be our master.

A life of self-imposed simplicity inspired by love, exemplified by St. Francis of Assisi and indeed by Pope Francis, is respected today, but the fact that no Western society produces enough children to maintain population levels must mean that many choose lifestyle and possessions rather than children, mammon rather than God.

Does this decision to have no children or few children impose extra pressures on a couple's faith, or does a weakened faith entail fewer children?

It is an interesting question. It helps demonstrate how we define the good life; how interested we are in searching for God and identifying his plans; and, most basically, whether we believe the Creator God exists and is good and interested in us.

Cardinal George Pell *is the prefect of the Vatican's Secretariat for the Economy.*

ELLEN T. CHARRY

"Which is greater: the gold, or the temple that makes the gold sacred?"

(MATTHEW 23:17)

Jesus was not a pretty character, according to Matthew. We meet an aggressive and angry Jesus in this section of Matthew's Gospel. His behavior is disorderly and disrespectful—disrupting normal business, killing a fig tree he disliked, heaping seven threatening "woes" against people whom he calls "blind guides" and "hypocrites" as well as six vicious parables, some of which threaten his opponents with death—and it precipitated his execution. Reading Matthew's account of the Jesus story, written perhaps 50 years after Jesus' death, it seems that Jesus brought his demise on himself, knowing full well what he was doing.

These two caustic rhetorical questions occur in Jesus' long diatribe against the scribes and Pharisees, which he began when he and his followers entered Jerusalem, the center of Jewish life:

> Woe to you, blind guides, who say, "Whoever swears by the sanctuary
> is bound by nothing, but whoever swears by the gold of the sanctuary is

bound by the oath." You blind fools! For which is greater, the gold or the
sanctuary that has made the gold sacred? And you say, "Whoever swears
by the altar is bound by nothing, but whoever swears by the gift that is on
the altar is bound by the oath." How blind you are! For which is greater,
the gift or the altar that makes the gift sacred? So whoever swears by the
altar, swears by it and by everything on it; and whoever swears by the sanc-
tuary, swears by it and by the one who dwells in it; and whoever swears by
heaven, swears by the throne of God and by the one who is seated upon it.
(Matthew 23:16–22, NRSV)

As rhetorical questions, their answers are assumed to be obvious.
The very nature of a rhetorical question is to shut the one questioned down into embarrassed silence. And Matthew's smear
campaign was successful. Two millennia of Christians have been
taught contempt for the Pharisees, these Jews from whom today's
Jews hail.

But just who were the objects of this denunciation, the scribes
and Pharisees on whom Jesus unleashed his ire, and who were the
priests, Levites and elders who were indicted by implication? Why
was this conflict so significant?

Scribes served the Jewish people as those learned in the law and
were often priests and Levites long before Jesus' day. They were
literate and by definition leaders on whom the people depended
for religious guidance. In Jesus' day, scribes would have been
responsible for copying, interpreting and translating Scripture
for worship. A blanket attack on "the scribes" is a denunciation of
educated leaders on whom the society depends.

The Pharisees were a small special-interest religious group in
ancient Palestine that emerged some 170 years before Jesus and
took over leadership after 70 C.E. when the Romans destroyed

the Jerusalem temple. The Apostle Paul identifies himself as among their number. Even before the catastrophe of 70 they were scrupulous adherents of biblical precepts, dedicated to applying commands found in Leviticus and other texts containing biblical law. They became more important after 70, when, as Jacob Neusner, a scholar of Judaism, has written, their dedication to Jewish purity—in the form of eating conventions, regulation of sex and other purity concerns—became the basis for Judaism's way forward.

Pharisaic piety works from the outside in. The principle is that what you do and do not do, and how you act and do not act, define you. Actualizing the community's mores and cultural patterns shapes and guides who you are. Something must go in in order for something to come out; we become what we know and what we do.

When the center of Jewish life and worship was destroyed by the Romans, Jews were in danger of assimilating into Greco-Roman culture and so away from the God of Scripture. Jesus, interpreted through Paul and the communities clustered around the evangelists, offered several ways of securing Judaism against extinction. The Pharisees offered another way, and this passage gives us a glimpse into their tight way of life devoted to obedience to God's precepts.

What can we glean from this passage? Matthew the evangelist has Jesus exposing his opponents' attempt to distinguish oaths that are to be taken more seriously from oaths that can be construed to carry weaker responsibilities. Jesus holds all oaths to be equally binding, while his opponents seem to recognize that we have conflicting responsibilities and must decide how to prioritize them. Christianity prizes love of neighbor. How are we to fulfill that obligation when family responsibilities press? How are we to care for family when that requires providing for children through a productive work life that may take one away from intimate contact?

Perhaps there is a word for us in this harsh diatribe. In situations of conflict, it is tempting to assume that we have the right answer and that our opponent has no real case to make. Denunciation becomes easier than reasoned argument. That is the very nature of a rhetorical question: the answer is assumed to be so obvious that a response is superfluous. But if we probe a bit, there may be reasons behind our opponent's position that escape us at first glance. There may even be something in that position worth considering.

Ellen T. Charry *is the Margaret W. Harmon Professor of Theology at Princeton Theological Seminary. Her latest book is a theological commentary on Psalms 1   50,* Sighs and Songs of Israel.

SISTER SIMONE CAMPBELL

"Why are you bothering this woman?"

(MATTHEW 26:10)

—•••—

Consider this scene: Jesus is in Bethany visiting the home of a man who suffers from a virulent skin disease. In his time, such folk were often considered unclean and rejected by society. It was also thought that they had done something wrong to deserve such punishment.

Into the room comes a woman with an alabaster jar of expensive ointment, who then proceeds to pour this oil over Jesus' head. Now, this is not a 21st century custom, but in that time it was an act of generosity and extravagance. It was a way of making fragrant a raw-stench world—the equivalent of being treated to a spa day or a stay at a five-star hotel. The woman gives Jesus a gift of abundance.

The men in the room start to grumble at the excess. They say, Why did Jesus let this happen? We could have sold the oil for a lot of money and given it to people who are poor! This would have been the noble (and not embarrassing) thing to do.

Jesus hears their grumbling and says to them, "Why are you bothering this woman?" What a good question!

As a Catholic sister, I want to ask the same question to the Vatican Congregation for the Doctrine of the Faith. In 2012, it issued a censure against the Leadership Conference of Women Religious, the association of leaders of more than 80% of U.S. Catholic sisters. It also named my little organization, NETWORK, as a problem. It said we were working too much with people in poverty, promoting radical feminist themes, and not working enough on its positions on abortion and gay marriage.

In the face of our mission and ministry, the men in the Vatican are grumbling. I want to ask them, Why are you bothering us while we pour out our lives in generosity for those who are often left out in our society? Why are you bothering us while we speak up for the needs of those left out of our economy? Why are you bothering us considering we have given our lives knowing the abundance of love showered on us?

I would also ask this follow-up question: Does our exuberance and generosity make you nervous?

I asked myself that often during NETWORK's Nuns on the Bus cross-country trip in the fall of 2014. Our 11-state trip was focused on getting "we the people" out to vote to help save our democracy from Big Money. On this journey, I saw much largesse and generosity—and I also saw how it made people uncomfortable.

At the United Church of Christ in Muskegon, Mich., volunteers serve breakfast every Saturday morning to an average of 350 people. However, they served more than 550 people the day we were there at the end of September.

Volunteers treated guests like servers at IHOP would, pouring coffee, caring for the kids and making sure everyone got what they needed. They have been doing this every Saturday since 2003, when they recognized the huge struggle that people in poverty face every day to put food on the table. The people from the church wanted to give struggling families a sense of relaxation and support. They pour out their care, but some nonchurch members from the neighborhood grumble that it is merely a drop in the bucket. These grumblers say the crowd is "disturbing the neighborhood" and "creating a Saturday-morning ruckus." I ask the grumblers, Why are you bothering these women (and, in this case, men)? They are pouring out their generosity in breakfast and cups of coffee.

In Flint, Mich., we went to St. Luke's N.E.W. Life Center and saw its amazing three-year program designed to help women develop leadership and self-esteem. It is run by two Catholic sisters, Sister Judy and Sister Carol.

We heard from Rhonda, a graduate of the program, who stands tall and speaks of what she has discovered about her skills and worth. Her favorite part of the program was the 40-day "love fest," an initiative to look in the mirror every day for 40 days and tell yourself everything that you like about what you see. During that time she learned how to appreciate her gifts, talents, beauty. She came to see her dignity and knew she could be a valued member of her community.

The sisters discovered that their graduates were having a hard time finding jobs, so they created N.E.W. Life Enterprises. It trains women to do commercial sewing, including making hospital scrubs and other cloth items. They also organized men for lawn and snow-removal businesses. These sisters and all of their colleagues are pouring out their care.

They are making new opportunities for many, and the way they are doing it creates opportunity for everyone. Yet they have struggles with buildings, zoning, opportunities, money, etc. Some grumblers tried to stop their work by saying a building they inhabit was a former elementary school and should not be used for adults or a business. These grumblers seem to fear change and are trying to stop it.

I ask the grumblers, Why are you bothering these women (and men)?

I have come to think that this question is a sign of how gifts and largesse make us nervous. I know that I can become uncomfortable when others overwhelm me with generosity. On our bus trip, a woman came up to me and gave me $5. She said she was unemployed and didn't have much but wanted to participate in our work. Her extravagance touched my heart, and I was tempted to give the money back. But in a flash I realized that she was doing the extravagant thing of caring for us. She, like the woman in the Gospel, was reaching out to another and showering her care.

Extravagance can be out of our control. Generous gifts can make us nervous. This may be why it is easier to criticize great generosity than to question whether we are called to it ourselves.

In this story in Matthew's Gospel, Jesus holds up a mirror and asks us to look deeply into ourselves. Am I someone who can let go of control and respond in generosity? Am I willing to reflect on those times when I grumble about another's gift giving? Am I willing to receive the largesse of another?

In short, when I start to grumble, am I willing to answer truthfully this probing question: Why are you bothering this woman?

Sister Simone Campbell *is the executive director of NETWORK, a Catholic social-justice lobby, and author of* A Nun on the Bus: How All of Us Can Create Hope, Change, and Community.

PHYLLIS TICKLE

> "Do you think I cannot call on my Father, and he will at once put at my disposal more than twelve legions of angels?"
>
> (MATTHEW 26:53)

The scene is so familiar that we hardly give it much pause nowadays, even if we are Christian and/or are deep into Eastertide. Jesus and the disciples have had their Last Supper and have gone out away from the city, ending up in the Garden of Gethsemane. There, if we are to believe Scripture, the disciples primarily sleep the time away, though Jesus himself prays. It is an easy scene to imagine, in no small part because we no longer have to. Hundreds of painters have already done that for us. Almost every Christian site has at least one centrally displayed example of the praying Christ and the naughty, sleeping followers.

What happens next has been almost as frequently represented

in art and certainly is almost as frequently displayed. The soldiers of the opposition come to seize and arrest Jesus. In the process, at least one disciple seems to rouse himself enough to grasp the situation and then to grasp his sword in defense of Jesus. He cuts off a soldier's ear—another delicious subject for visual artists—an action for which he is immediately chastised. Jesus restores the severed ear, even as he corrects his disciple.

Not only artists, both good and bad, but also preachers, both good and bad, love this story. Certainly, for all of us the principle of pacifism is anchored here, though it has received more lip service than adherence in the centuries since. And even more certainly, the whole paradoxical submission of God to the schemes and evil of humanity in order to effect the plan of God for the sake of humanity is rich and terrifying territory. It is also, of course, theologically central to any engagement with the meaning of Calvary and the Christian doctrine of atonement, which makes it a bit of a homiletic necessity, whether one wishes it were or not.

But what has always gotten lost in this—what has fascinated me since childhood and perhaps, truth be told, even undone me at times—is that simple but central question that is stuck, like an errant chord, right smack dab in the middle of it all: Do you think I cannot call on my Father, and he will at once put at my disposal more than twelve legions of angels?

Or better said, what undoes me and has for years is the question, "Do I?"

Do I really think that there were legions of angels gathered there, waiting to be called to the rescue?

Really?

If so, then oh, my God, have mercy on me, a sinner!

But if not—if indeed I think not—I must unsay my own

Scriptures not only here but in literally dozens of places. Certainly, I must unsay those pages which tell us that it is angels who announced the conception of the God-man whom I worship. And if there are no angels, then I must also look askance at the pages of Scripture that say it was angels who, in due time, heralded his birth. More poignantly, I must deny those sections that tell me about the angels who ministered to him in the desert of his preparation. And most painful of all, if there are no angels, then I must abandon forever the angelic cries of glory at his Resurrection; and after that, their holy instruction to his still earthbound followers after his ascension. In sum, then, and long before his coming into our time and space, the Scripture that foretells and prepares us for him is rife with angels. Everywhere and always, angels.

And what is that about? What are we to make of such almost un-self-conscious insistence, not only in Christian and Jewish Scripture but in the wisdom literature and holy writings of all peoples across all time, that there are angels? Or if not angels per se, then for lack of a better term, that there are divinely orchestrated interveners and messengers and agents which operate within our sphere but are not yet subject to our descriptive comprehension or analysis? What if we do indeed, as our forebears have all said and as the Christ, facing his own submission to torture and death, dares us to believe ... what if we do indeed live within an angel-inhabited cosmos?

I don't know the answer to that question. If I did, I probably would not be writing this small essay, for it really is a cry for help, isn't it? It really is a kind of plea, in fact, that we—or at least some of us—might begin to talk nonmythologically about what it means, in the 21st century, to live in an angel-infused, angel-inhabited life. And conversely, of course, what it could and perhaps does mean to continue to live in denial of the fact that ours is such a world. What, in a cosmos that increasingly is rendering up its mechanistic and mechanical wonders and machinations, does it mean to live as creatures of both a physical and an extraphysical or transphysical milieu? Even within my own Christian faith, ancient and liturgically rich communions like Orthodoxy and Roman Catholicism steer clear of addressing such questions as that directly, much less contemporaneously.

But even after all of that, there is still and always that haunting question, isn't there? Do you think I cannot call on my Father, and he will at once put at my disposal more than twelve legions of angels?

The question, especially in its Gethsemane context, leads me to the much more quotidian question of: How now, Lord, shall I pray? How carefully? How cautiously and how submissively? Are there really those of your appointment who can effect my words?

And if so, may the God of Gethsemane have mercy on us, sinners all ...

Phyllis Tickle *is the founding editor of the religion department of Publishers Weekly and the author of many books, including the* Divine Hours *manuals on fixed prayer.*

LUKE POWERY

"My God, my God, why have you forsaken me?"

(MATTHEW 27:46)

—•••—

"Jesus cried with a loud voice, '*Eli, Eli, lema sabachthani?*,' that is, "My God, my God, why have you forsaken me?" A cry from the Christ on a Cross. Not a three-point sermon ending with a poem. A cry. Jesus doesn't quote Karl Barth's *Church Dogmatics* or John Calvin's *Institutes* or Dietrich Bonhoeffer's *Life Together* or *Chicken Soup for the Soul* at this point of desperation. Here the word of God quotes the word of God. This cry of lament comes from Psalm 22, and in the mouth of Jesus it can't be avoided even if we want to ignore it. It is a cry that still echoes loudly down the acoustical corridors of church history—"My God, my God, why have you forsaken me?"

It is a cry of lament, forsakenness and abandonment. The contemporary text message might be, OMG WTF? This may not make you comfortable, but the cry from a Cross shouldn't make anyone comfortable. We in the church can be socialized liturgical zombies and get caught up in fancy phrases like "when the praises go up, the blessings come down." But Jesus shows us another doxological posture before God because what do you do when the praises go up and cancer comes down? What do you do when the praises go up and depression takes up residence in your life without paying rent? What do you do when the praises go up but you hear God crying out to God, "My God, my God, why have you forsaken me?" It almost seems as if God has given up on Godself. What do you do when Good Friday is every day and Jesus is on crucified lockdown about to be executed on a bloody death row? What do you do when you have to bear a cross alone? I'll tell you what to do—lament, cry, moan, groan and lament some more.

Some have tried to sanitize and bleach the blood of the Cross and hang a nice, little, safe, pretty, mute Jesus around their neck. But the cry from the Cross continues with or without us. Jesus cries for all the innocent men and women who are being lynched, crucified on contemporary crosses today. Jesus cries out from a wooden tree for all of us who ask, "Why?"

Lament is faithful speech, and one-third of the book of Psalms contains lament psalms. And the loud outcry of lament continues today in our world in the cries of black men killed by weapons of violence. Do you hear the cries of Trayvon Martin, Michael Brown, Eric Garner and Tamir Rice? Do you hear "Help!" "Don't shoot!" "I can't breathe!"? My God, my God, why?! Modern-day crucifixions of American citizens in Sanford, Fla.; Ferguson, Mo.; Staten Island, N.Y.; and Cleveland—all guilty of walking while black. My God, my God, why? They cried out loud.

They were crucified in Golgotha, USA. Golgotha, the place of the skull, is not at the top of the list of summer-vacation destinations. Golgotha is not where a pastor wants to begin a new church. The cry from a tree on Golgotha's hill is an indictment of the way life is. This expression of lament, according to Old Testament scholar Walter Brueggemann, basically declares, "Life is not right!"

Jesus' cry critiques the norm, so the religious and political powers of the day attempt to kill the cry of Jesus. Jesus' final melody is in the tune of a Psalm 22 loud cry of lament, that same lament that ethics scholar and United Theological Seminary of the Twin Cities president Barbara Holmes says "danced and swayed" in the belly of the slave ships of the Middle Passage. What else can you do on a cross under the weight of suffering? But lament! "My God, my God, why have you forsaken me?"

Jesus may not be wearing a hoodie, but he's bearing a cross. He shows us the consequence of a prophetic mission. He shows us that giving oneself to God does not mean success, prosperity or even popularity. In the words of theologian and civil rights leader Howard Thurman, Jesus shows us "the logic of what happens to love in the world." But even as Jesus goes down to death, he's not going by himself. That loud cry will have the last laugh, shaking the very foundations of the world.

The lament of Psalm 22 on the lips of Jesus moves as many lament psalms do—from plea to praise or hope. It begins with the cry of lament but transitions and concludes with "Posterity will serve him; future generations will be told about the Lord, and proclaim his deliverance to a people yet unborn, saying that he has done it." Lament does not make its bed in a pool of silent tears but raises its voice before God for deliverance, trusting God to act faithfully. "Jesus cried again with a loud voice and breathed his last. At that moment the curtain of the temple was torn in two, from top to bottom."

The loud cry of Jesus causes the temple to crumble. Completely, totally, entirely, fully demolished. His loud cry decenters the center of the religious order and rips oppression apart. His loud cry establishes another order as he ends his life with fighting words. Through a loud cry all sanctioned religious segregation was destroyed. His loud cry opens up access to the divine. No longer divisions between profane and sacred. All have access to God through the death of Jesus. He cried and died and starts a new era and a new way. One simple cry tore up the whole system! No guns, no tanks, no shoe bombs, no knives. A cry of lament that shakes the earth, splits rocks and opens tombs. When Jesus cries and dies, something has to change. When Jesus cries and dies, something new has to rise. His death kills the way we kill each other in the name of God. His death is not really his end but the end of destructive ways of human life.

So don't underestimate the loud cry of Jesus, because it is that cry that opens up God's future for us and gives us access to God's presence in the world and our lives. You shouldn't underestimate a loud cry of lament, because as New Testament scholar Clifton Black wrote, "the spine of lament is hope." Don't underestimate a cry. That cry of Christ is creating a new reality, from top to bottom.

So cry out because even when you cry in anguish, "My God, my God," God is still present in the cry. Cry out loud until death and mourning are no more. Cry out loud until new systems and structures are put in place to protect the innocent and convict the guilty. Cry out loud until the "new Jim Crow" prison-industrial complex is destroyed. Cry out loud against hatred of any kind. Cry out loud until the wolf lies down with the lamb. Cry out loud to and for Jesus. Because Jesus cried out, we can learn that even interrogatory lament is worship of God. So cry out!

Luke Powery *is the dean of Duke University Chapel and an associate professor of homiletics at Duke Divinity School.*

JOEL HOUSTON

"Which is easier: to say to this paralyzed man, 'Your sins are forgiven,' or to say, 'Get up, take your mat and walk'?"

(MARK 2:9)

·•·

Blaise Pascal, the French mathematician and philosopher who died in 1662, said, "Man's sensitivity to small things, and his insensitivity to the most important things, are surely evidences of a strange disorder." English theologian G.K. Chesterton observed nearly three centuries later that big things sometimes have a better way of hiding than small things, and he used the shape of the earth to illustrate his point—that for years we thought the earth was flat, but its true form was hidden by both its size and ours.

Perhaps most of us would agree with Pascal and Chesterton in that there exists in our world a "strange order"—that both the size of great things and confusion about what is great prohibit us from living life in a sort of spiritual awareness. I find I am often victim to the backwardness of this culture when an NBA trade catches my attention and rouses the emotions as I pass quickly over the smaller headline of a genocide in Sudan.

The sin of the world is a thing that is very large—almost obvious—but very distant at times. Our own sin is very close but seemingly manageable and not as dark as the distant, more depraved sin of the online beheader or the murdering militant. Perhaps it takes personal disaster or disability to come to terms with the real problem of brokenness in the world. When we have a friend who is going through torment, we begin to peek our heads out of our intentional distraction and come to terms with the plight of the human situation.

It is precisely within this context that Jesus asked questions 2,000 years ago to a crowded house full of the sick and sinful, who were surrounded by saints and skeptics.

"What is easier, to forgive this man his sins or to heal him?"

If I were in that room, I would be wondering how one can even measure forgiveness to begin with. How do we know someone has been forgiven? How can that claim even be substantiated? It's not like we can hold the human soul up to a blue light and check it for stains. Is there an X-ray machine that can detect the legal standing of a spirit? In my mind, seeing a known paralytic man be physically healed would be much more impressive because that could be observed and measured. It would fall under the certainty of the scientific method—healing on demand, on command.

This type of proposition that Jesus puts forward is an argument in logic called *a fortiori* (Latin for "with stronger reason"). It goes like this: if I can lift this table, then obviously I can lift this banana. The weightier thing in their eyes was to heal the man. After his question, Jesus healed the man to prove his authority to forgive sins.

The healing ultimately posed another question to everyone in the room: What do you do with the hard evidence? If Jesus heals this man, what conclusions do I draw when presented with this irrefutable evidence?

Miracles—even the miracles of Jesus—are still a much debated topic within Christianity. I find it very difficult to separate Jesus from his miracles because of stories like this—Jesus used miracles to demonstrate his power over nature, demons, sickness, death and that much heavier yet intangible human cancer, sin. But we are faced with another dilemma regarding miracles, and that is this: miracles don't equate with biblical faith.

Some may ask, "If God is God, why does he take such great care in hiding himself?" James, Jesus' younger brother, wrote that even the demons "believe and tremble." On one side there exist those who are not satisfied with God's lack of visibility; on the other side, there are those who are fully aware of God's existence, power and ability and still refuse to trust him.

So then is it possible to see God, or see miracles, and not have saving faith? Absolutely. Hebrews 3 reminds us that the children of Israel—who saw the 10 plagues of Egypt, the parting of the Red Sea, the pillar of fire and pillar of cloud and many other miracles— died of unbelief. How can people see miracles, or know that God exists, yet still harden their hearts toward him?

The journey of humanity toward God is not a journey of the eyes but rather of the heart. The eyes of the paralytic's friends saw a long journey carrying a stretcher, a friend unable to believe for himself, a house crowded with no room for them and a perfectly good roof that shouldn't be damaged. But their hearts had decided who Jesus was, and they would do anything to get their friend to him that day.

I am reminded again of Jesus' great humility in the story too. Unafraid of the skeptic or the religious elite, he answers their questions and heals a man in the middle of their active unbelief. For all we know, the paralytic may have been the one with the most unbelief. Maybe that was his sin. But we know from Mark's Gospel that it was the faith of the paralytic's friends in Jesus that healed him. Many people are often put off by Jesus because they have their doubts. Jesus doesn't seem limited by anyone's doubts in this story. If anything, he works miracles in the shade of doubts.

Still Jesus shows even more humility, both in the receiving of the man, in the seeing past his paralysis to his friends, past the doubt of the crowd and ultimately to the revealing of his personhood. The proud often refrain from explaining themselves, dodging questions from people they consider to be unworthy or unable to understand. A fool may utter all his mind, but the humble doesn't mind being mistaken for a fool.

A final mark of Christ's great humility can be seen in his self-disclosure to everyone who was present in the room. He was not put off by the "doubting Thomas" or his modern counterpart, skeptical Susan. And he still asks the same question today, in unparalleled humility: "What is easier—to fix you, or to forgive you?" There is no doubt that the world needs fixing, but isn't the more obvious and paradoxically hidden truth that the world needs to be forgiven?

Joel Houston *is a songwriter and pastor. He leads the Sydney-based band Hillsong United.*

BISHOP MINERVA G. CARCAÑO

"How can the guests of the bridegroom fast while he is with them?"

(MARK 2:19)

—•••—

When I was a child, nothing delighted me quite like the visit of our pastor at family meals. Sometimes our pastor came for Sunday lunch, sometimes for our birthday picnics, sometimes even on Thanksgiving Day. My family was a faithful churchgoing family but not what was considered a prominent family in the church. We were a poor family living on the outskirts of Edinburg, Texas, subsisting on picking cotton, packing fruit and vegetables for shipment at the local produce company, at best working the lowest-wage entry-level jobs. Prominence even at our church required money and social status, neither of which we had. So when our pastor came to share a meal with us, our lives were transformed from insignificance to being special! Even as a child I understood that our pastor was a representative of God and I could feel the presence of God as our pastor came to be with us.

My grandmother Sofia and my mother Rebecca fasted during

high holy days and when the family faced a crisis, but the visit of our pastor was never a time to fast. The best food we had would be prepared in abundance, no one thinking about what we would eat the next day. We would sit for hours at that dining-room table, enjoying the food, but even more, enjoying the presence of our pastor, who told us stories of faith, making them come alive. He would ask about our lives, always assuring us that we were not alone because God was with us. We would laugh at life's struggles and at our own frailties, because after all, God loved us just as we were, and God was on our side!

The next day, we would return to the ordinary, the mundane and life's struggles. Faith in God who loved us and chose to be with us sustained us. Sacred memories of being at the table with God's messenger encouraged us. Those childhood experiences of truly spiritual banquets would become formative in my life. They shaped my understanding of God and what it meant to be a disciple of Jesus.

The passage from the Gospel according to Mark about Jesus and his disciples feasting at the table of Levi and others makes me remember my pastor's visits. I don't think my pastor would have been offended to hear me say today that I count what my family and I experienced with him as but a fraction of what those who received Jesus into their homes must have felt when he came among them to share a meal, to share life and to share a blessing. What joy must have filled their hearts! The Son of God, the very incarnation of God, right there with them because God loved them and was on their side!

But joy isn't everyone's experience. When leaders from my church would hear of the pastor coming to our home to share a meal with us, they would often be displeased. Criticism would arise in a variety of ways, but the bottom line was always why the pastor would waste his time with us. Shouldn't he have been praying, studying the Bible, preparing a sermon, fasting instead of feasting with the likes of us? It's interesting how the practice of religion can create doubt even when expressed through good and righteous acts. It's a sign of how we through our own interpretations can corrupt what is sacred, sometimes confusing even those who want to believe.

John the Baptist and his disciples fasted. The Pharisees fasted. But when people looked Jesus' way, what they saw was Jesus and his disciples feasting with people rather than fasting. It was confusing to know what to believe. What were they to believe? Their question prompted a question back from Jesus: "The wedding guests cannot fast while the bridegroom is with them, can they?"

No! If God loves us and chooses to come and abide among us, how can we fast? It would be as if we were fasting while a wedding was going on. If we fasted at a wedding, wouldn't the message be that we were not pleased by the wedding? Wouldn't it be a sign that perhaps we didn't approve of the wedding or the marriage? Fasting would not be an appropriate response at a wedding, a time meant for joy. If God comes to us to shower upon our lives his own love and sustaining mercy and grace, is that not surely a time to feast and celebrate and not fast?

There are moments when fasting is appropriate, but can we strive to allow the very best of our humanity to determine when we fast and when we rejoice, the very humanity we see in Jesus? Jesus knows how broken we are, and he comes among us in just the way we need. My family and I needed to know that we were worthy of being loved in a society and even a church that considered us to be inferior and unworthy. We were not perfect people, but knowing that God was the loving and merciful safety net of our lives allowed us to trust God with the totality of our sinful lives. Today we strive to practice the religious disciplines of our Christian faith while also trying to faithfully embody and share the love of Jesus who one good day met us right where we were.

The best news of all is that Jesus brings God's love to all of us without exception. Isn't that worth setting aside fasting for rejoicing?

Minerva G. Carcaño *is the United Methodist Bishop for the Los Angeles Area, which spans Southern California, Hawaii, Guam and Saipan.*

"Which is lawful on the Sabbath: to do good or to do evil, to save life or to kill?"

(MARK 3:4)

—•••—

We are not called to serve religion; religion is called to serve humanity. Anything else is oppression.

Jesus got this question when his disciples plucked corn on the Sabbath, driven by hunger.

Christ's answer was that "the Sabbath was made for man, not man for the Sabbath."

As important as the Sabbath was for Jews, an established commandment and a cultural linchpin of Hebrew life, Jesus' words displayed a foundational, divine truth that love trumps law.

If your ox falls into a ditch on the Sabbath, you get the ox out of the ditch, not just because you need the ox but also because the ox needs you. It is right and holy to do good at all times.

Love is the spiritual imperative that overrides any law.

I believe the question posed raises Martin Luther King Jr.'s concept of the "beloved community." What is the beloved community? What does the beloved community look, taste and feel like? It is certainly not a place where religious traditions are more important than the law of love.

Oppressive religion, or a theology that welcomes those who fit a normative definition of the dominant culture while excluding those who do not, is a ball and chain on the heart of the message of Jesus. Jesus was a scandal, a political subversive who spoke truth to power and liberty to those in bondage. Any theology that suggests that God receives some and rejects others is not reflective of the ministry of Jesus Christ.

Jesus, the son of a young Jewish mother, raised by a blue collar carpenter, welcomed, included and healed the broken, outcast and needy. Jesus healed people to remove their stigma and to return them to productivity. Jesus stood with the men in his home synagogue, read from the scroll of Isaiah one Sabbath morning and said:

> *The Spirit of the Lord is on me, because he has anointed me to proclaim good news to the poor. He has sent me to proclaim freedom for the prisoners and recovery of sight for the blind, to set the oppressed free, to proclaim the year of the Lord's favor. (Luke 4:18–19)*

These priorities must also be the priorities of an oppression-free beloved community. How can we be the church of Jesus unless we reflect the ministry and heart of Jesus? Is the church a radical incarnation of the ministry of Jesus or a private social club? It is crucial in the formation of community that those who were and are oppressed seek to overcome the theological millstones tied around their necks. It is equally important not to adopt pejorative assumptions toward others in community who are different and thus pass on the sickness of an oppressive theology.

This inherited and promoted oppression leads to stereotyping for the purpose of gaining power or advantage. Donald Chinula, using King's notion of the beloved community, asserts that oppression manifested as an unjust use of authority or advantage "seeks its own advantage at the expense of the oppressed and strives to perpetuate itself." Stereotyping allows the oppressor to stand apart from the oppressed and categorize and pigeonhole a group of people. This oppression is particularly insidious when the religion is used to defend it.

We all need community. When access to existing communities is not available, marginalized people must seek to develop community for and among themselves. Where people are giving birth to a fresh, emerging Christian community, old barriers exist and must be overcome.

The theology of those at the center of society often seeks to characterize people on the edge as enemies of God. This is especially true when individuals or groups unrepentantly refuse to conform to the dominant definition of normativity. Overcoming internal and external oppressive theology, or a theology that excludes certain people, is primary in creating a Christian community for people visibly on the periphery.

Those who promote theologies that exclude certain races, cultures, sexual and gender orientations and classes in the name of Jesus would do well to remember that Jesus was himself from the edge of society with a ministry to those who were considered least.

Marginalized people, now as in the time of Jesus' earthly ministry, respond to a community of openness and inclusivity, where other people from the edge gather. Such an atmosphere welcomes people to feel it is safer to be who they are. A liberating theology of acceptance must be embodied in the atmosphere of a liberating

Christian community. Contempt for the church and all things religious often stems from exposure to oppressive theology, biblical literalism and unyielding tradition. A person, church or society can do extreme harm when that harm is done in the name of God and virtue and with the "support" of Scripture. In *The Good Book,* Peter Gomes reflects on an old aphorism he heard from a friend: "A surplus of virtue is more dangerous than a surplus of vice, because a surplus of virtue is not subject to the constraints of conscience."

I heard a story the other day about an incredible Jewish woman, Naomi, who feels called to serve people who are ravaged by Alzheimer's disease. She was seeking to help an African-American woman, Gladys, who loved to sing gospel music before Alzheimer's afflicted her. This loving Jewish woman knew what to do to ignite the life in Gladys. She began to sing songs about Jesus, and the light came on in her patient's eyes. It did not matter that their religions espoused doctrines and beliefs that suggested their faith had no common denominator. They were together enfolded in the arms of a loving God, and love trumped law once again!

Yvette Flunder *is the Presiding Bishop of the Fellowship of Affirming Ministries headquartered in Oakland, Calif.*

KATE BRAESTRUP

"How can Satan drive out Satan?"

(MARK 3:23)

––•••––

Psychosis is the medical term for when a mentally ill person's disconnection from reality is complete, but *bonkers* is a less scary word than *psychotic.*

"My baby is bonkers," my friend Susan told me over the phone. Her daughter Freya, hallucinating and delusional, had been taken to the emergency room by the police. Because she isn't actually a baby but a young adult, when Freya forbade hospital personnel to call her mother, they were honor-bound—or rather, HIPAA-bound—to obey. Even if in the same breath, Freya was declaring herself a conjoined twin addicted to angel dust and a close friend of the Dalai Lama.

I helped Susan track Freya down. It took three days. Thanks to the doctors who talked her into going to a mental hospital for treatment, Susan and I found Freya safe and, if not sound, at least sheltered, fed, medicated … and bonkers.

"She's signed a release form," the psychiatrist said. "So we can share her medical details with you."

Later, Freya told us she had had no idea what this form was. "I thought they were asking for my kidneys," she said. She's a generous person. She signed.

"Possessed by demons" is what they called mental illness back in Bible days, and when someone you've known since her infancy gazes mystified at you with her familiar eyes, and in her familiar voice says strange, senseless things, the impression is definitely that something else has taken possession.

Freya was lucky. She hadn't taken angel dust. Indeed, she avoided drugs and alcohol throughout her adolescence and in so doing dodged the most common, lethal complication of her illness.

Susan was lucky. She is a relatively well-educated person. She knew there were scientific explanations for what was happening. Her daughter was getting the best care possible. And still Susan was terrified.

The Bible was never meant to be a sort of 1st century *Physicians' Desk Reference*. However, since both Jewish and Christian Scripture are devoted primarily to considering human life and relationships, anything commonly encountered in life tends to turn up in its pages as the authors struggle to convey the essence and identity of God.

After years in seminary, I know who God is. *God is love.* It sounds so simple! Yet we've been struggling to fully grasp its implications for millennia. We don't always know just how or whom to love, and still we are called to do it. The command is absolute and implacable: *love one another.*

So how does the God who is love regard mental illness? What does Jesus—love incarnate, according to the story—do when confronted with someone who is … bonkers?

The Gospels offer many examples, but perhaps the most vivid is the Gerasene demoniac (Mark 5).

Exiled by a community that does not know how to help him, the Gerasene behaves as many mentally ill people do today if left uncared for or unmedicated. The poor man raves naked among the tombs, injuring himself and howling.

"Freya is not like that," Susan said fiercely as we rode the elevator down from the secure floor after our first visit. "She's *not*." I put my arms around her, wishing, not for the first time, that I had more to offer.

There were other, and much sicker, patients in the hospital, and there are other mentally ill characters in the Bible too. Whether or not you believe in Jesus' miracles, what the healing stories undoubtedly illustrate is our longing for health, and not only for ourselves. We long to see others made well: our loved ones, neighbors and strangers. Love yearns to restore the blind man's sight and the leper's skin and would make whole the madman's broken mind.

Bonkers, Freya remained in the hospital. Susan and I visited every afternoon. It was hard. She knew who her mom was, more or less, but Freya didn't know who she was.

She had theories. She was the designer of the building, a doctor doing research or maybe an undercover police officer. The nurses were CIA agents watching her with miniature cameras, drugging her food or hiding her babies from her.

After each visit, Susan and I drove to a nearby restaurant, noticing with too much clarity the mentally ill homeless people suffering in the streets. Susan would eat supper without tasting it. I would try to talk her out of despair.

"She's complying with treatment," the nurses assured us. "That's the good news. She's such a sweet young woman!"

When Jesus meets the Gerasene demoniac, he is not complying with treatment.

This is important, because in the Gospels, Jesus' healings are often initiated by the sick people themselves.

"All I have to do is touch the hem of his garment," a woman with an issue of blood says to herself. She reaches out, touches Jesus as he passes by, and the blood stops flowing. Jesus says, "*Your faith has made you whole.*"

Those possessed by demons don't choose healing. Their choice machine is broken. Their faith machine is broken too; if anything, the demons within the Gerasene energetically resist Jesus' intervention in a way an emergency-room psychiatrist might recognize. "What do you have to do with me? Stay away from me! *You're from the CIA!*"

Jesus heals him anyway. Jesus doesn't say, "Your faith has made you whole." The demoniac couldn't make himself whole. He couldn't reach out for help and healing. Help and healing had to reach out for him.

A meeting had been scheduled for the sixth day of Freya's hospitalization. Her doctors told Susan that as an adult with the right to make her own health care choices, Freya would be present at the meeting. Susan shook her head.

"Freya's rights are a fiction," she said angrily. "It will be a meeting between four relatively sane people all pretending not to notice that the fifth is nucking futs."

What Susan and I didn't know, however, was that as of the sixth day, the lithium in Freya's system had reached its therapeutic threshold. Freya walked into the meeting room a little dazed, but she was herself.

With her familiar eyes, she looked at her mother and in her familiar voice said, "Hi, Mom."

"Oh my God." Susan burst into tears.

And when the people came and saw the demoniac sitting there, clothed and in his right mind, they were afraid.

Afraid, I gazed at Freya, hardly daring to speak in case a word might somehow tip her back into the abyss. But no. There she was, loving and beloved, an undivided self again.

Lithium is not a cure. Barring some breakthrough in treatment for bipolar disorder, Freya will take medication for the rest of her life. Still, like the sufferers in the Gospels, like the Gerasene who was no longer a demoniac but could instead be called a disciple, Freya has been healed and freed to plan a life of service. She shall be a witness for love among the people.

Kate Braestrup *is a Unitarian Universalist minister and the chaplain to the Maine Warden Service. She is the author of* Anchor and Flares: A Memoir of Motherhood, Hope, and Service.

YOLANDA PIERCE

"What is your name?"

(MARK 5:9)

—•••—

I recently observed a veteran kindergarten teacher during her morning routine. First she greeted each child at the door. After the students had put away their belongings in their individually labeled cubbies, she took a verbal roll call. She called each student by his or her full name—first, middle, last—their serious adult names that their 5-year-old bodies had yet to grow into. And each child, apparently accustomed to the routine, answered her with a firm "Present." I left the classroom thinking about what it means for someone to call us by our full names. What does it mean for someone to know our name and to care that we are present when our name is called?

The story told in the first half of the Gospel of Mark, Chapter 5, is best known for how Jesus interacts with and heals the man from Gerasenes who was demon-possessed, but it is ultimately a story about the power of naming names. The "demon-possessed" man knows exactly who Jesus is, naming him: "Jesus, Son of the Most High God." And while the man is in the process of begging

Jesus not to torment him, Jesus asks a question to which he surely already knew the answer: "What is your name?" It is this question, and not necessarily the answer that the man gives, that reveals the true lesson of this story.

Names in the ancient world carried great value and importance, for not only did a name identify someone, it frequently expressed the essential nature of its bearer; in other words, to know the name was to know the person. To know a name was to also have access to a genealogy or family history; a name revealed crucial information about one's origins and background. When Jesus asks the Gerasene his name, he provokes the man to identify his true nature and essence, to proclaim how he understands himself. When the man answers that his name is "Legion," the reader knows that not only has he forgotten his true name but also that his very identity has become his demon-possessed condition. The term *legion* refers to, using military language, the various conflicts and inner turmoil that had so afflicted him that he had been shackled in chains and forced to live apart from his community. These inner demons were so great in number that they were like a Roman military force encamped within his soul. So when the Gerasene answers that his name is "Legion," we know that this is a man who has lost everything—his identity, his family history, his friends and his true name.

This question, "What is your name?," prompts the verbal identification of those forces that had stolen this man's joy, peace and sanity. The legion may refer to a set of social forces and hierarchies, which could have created an overwhelming sense of despair within him. The legion may be the ravages of a mental illness, a condition for which the ancient world had no cure or understanding. The contemporary reader of this ancient text is invited to think about what is legion in his or her life. We are invited to name our fears, our sins and our troubled interior places, along with naming those structural sins, injustices and oppressions that create broken bodies and fractured minds, dehumanize and obscure identities. When Jesus asks the Gerasene "What is your name?," he begins the first step in the healing process: naming that which has caused the harm. The first step in the work of healing, reconciliation and restoration is to name names.

This man, the story tells us, walked around a graveyard day and night, howling and bruising himself with stones, constantly wrenching his shackles and breaking his chains. He has been ostracized from his village and condemned as ritually unclean and therefore not worthy of being integrated back into his community. His family has abandoned him, and no one is able to subdue him or even get close enough to comfort him. And yet he is still worthy of attention from Jesus. While Jesus sees the man's distressing condition, by asking for his name, Jesus sees beyond the man's physical circumstances and psychological state. Jesus affirms that this confused man is still someone worthy of dignity, respect and restoration to his rightful name and identity. By the end of the story, the man who is known in the biblical text only by his condition, "the Gerasene demoniac," is made whole and restored to his community, proclaiming the good news of what Jesus has done. While the reader never learns his rightful name, we do learn that respect and dignity have been restored to him.

By thinking about the question Jesus poses in Mark 5:9, we can shift our attention away from the behavior of so-called demon possession and onto the healing and restoration possible when someone who has lost everything and everyone is finally seen as fully human and still worthy of love and recognition. There is a promise of God found in the Old Testament book of Isaiah: "I have called you by name, you are mine." When Jesus asks "What is your name?," he echoes this promise that everyone, irrespective of his or her physical or mental condition, is known, called and embraced by God.

I think about the kindergarten class I observed and the care the teacher took to call each child by his or her full name. There will be times in the future of each of those children when someone will call them harmful names, names that wound, names that diminish their humanity and dignity. Some of those children will face a future in which they will be pejoratively labeled merely on the basis of race or creed or gender.

I hope they will remember a teacher who cared enough to start each day with a reminder of the names they were given out of love.

Yolanda Pierce *is the director of the Center for Black Church Studies and an associate professor of African-American Religion and Literature at Princeton Theological Seminary.*

WILFREDO DE JESÚS

"Who touched my clothes?"

(MARK 5:30)

...

There is tremendous power in human touch. And yet research shows that Americans tend to be a bit touch-phobic. According to *Psychology Today,* healthy human touch induces oxytocin, the "bonding hormone," which is renowned for reducing stress, lowering cortisol levels and increasing a sense of trust and security. This gives a whole new meaning to the words *healing touch*. Jesus, the Great Physician, understood the incredible divine potential in human contact to the extent that in Mark 5:30, he poses a question that makes him seem, at first, a bit haphephobic himself.

Surrounded by a crushing crowd, rushing to aid a gravely ill child, Jesus suddenly stops dead in his tracks. He turns to the mob and asks, Who touched me? He must have asked this in an authoritative tone, because the Luke account says everyone denies doing so. While the question is clearly odd, the denial is absurd. They were all pressing in around him. Immediately, we can sense his urgency in unveiling the culprit. I imagine that the disciples began to hold up their hands in denial and slowly back away. In defensiveness, they start to critique the motive of his inquisition. But

Jesus won't let the issue drop; in fact, he becomes more persistent with their resistance.

Every word, every moment, every encounter in Jesus' life is strategic. Hidden behind the hem of his cloak is a divine appointment.

"Who touched me?" The answer was a social taboo: a woman. If that wasn't enough, she was also bleeding. For 12 years, the story tells us, she suffered from an incurable condition, the nature of which would have brought shame and ridicule associated with punishment for sin. This made her ritually unclean, which was basically religious and medical quarantine. She would have been an outcast who had a responsibility to know her place on the outskirts of town. She likely was expected to cry out "Unclean!" when in earshot of others to warn them of her approach.

As a woman, bleeding and diseased, she was a triple threat. Her presence in the crowd in itself was an affront to decency and custom. She would have had to go to great lengths to conceal herself enough to get anywhere near Jesus. For 12 years, everyone, everywhere, everything with which she came in contact was considered contaminated by her touch. She was defined by her nameless disease. Even 2,000 years later, she remains nameless—known and remembered as the woman with the issue of blood. The isolation would have been maddening; surely she longed to be normal, to fit in with the crowd.

Who is this woman? Her audacity, her persistence, her relentless pursuit of an answer is inspiring. The Gospel writer says "she had suffered a great deal under the care of many doctors and had spent all she had, yet instead of getting better she grew worse." Most of us would have long since thrown in the towel. Exposing herself to experimental treatments like a human guinea pig, she grew worse and wound up flat broke. In spite of these fearful odds, she never loses hope. Her faith drives her into Jesus' presence, because she thinks, "If I just touch his clothes, I will be healed" (Mark 5:28).

And healed she was, but in more ways than she expected. With the same tenacity that she pursues Jesus, he pursues her. Just as Jesus is the sole answer to her prayers, she is the only person who can answer his question: Who touched me?

His question demands an answer—and gives her a voice. In spite of her quest to blend in, he calls her out of the crowd. Jesus elevates her for her amazing faith. She painfully confesses her secret suffering and hidden healing. Her testimony glorifies God, and the truth sets her free from the stigma she carried. "Daughter, your faith has healed you," Jesus says. "Go in peace and be freed from your suffering."

She is no longer a prodigal but a daughter. She is reminded of her place in the family, of the unconditional love of her heavenly Father. With a simple question, Jesus provokes her from fear to faith, from guilt to glory, from pain to peace. With a simple touch, the woman is healed from a lifetime of open emotional, physical and spiritual wounds. The edge of a cloak flips her world upside down.

Often, as Christians, we feel the need to have all the answers. We spend money on the newest books and fancy programs. We recruit the best theological experts to find a cure for the moral and spiritual ills around us. In reality, all the world needs is God's presence—those who would push through the crowd will surely find healing. Instead of answers, we might do better to pose questions, like: Who has touched Jesus? The testimonies that follow might just turn our world upside down.

Wilfredo De Jesús *is the pastor of New Life Covenant Church in Chicago.*

MIHEE KIM-KORT

"Why all this commotion and wailing?"

(MARK 5:39)

It is a rare moment when all three of them are yelling for something at the same time. Ozzie—named after the fiery evangelist Oswald Chambers—is still in a bellowing stage. The twins, Desmond and Anna, tend to plead their cases with me like I am judge and jury with their voices increasing in volume as they make their demands. I get whiplash from trying to make sense of their jumbled words and Ozzie's periodic yelping as he gets a word in edgewise. When all three go at it I feel like I'm in a bizarre chamber of horrors. I can run, and I can hide, but unfortunately not for long. They always, always find me.

The commotion of our daily lives—it's rooted in the arbitrarily popular-for-three-seconds toys and natural assertion of human bodies to carve out space whether they are 3 ft. tall or 6 ft. 3 in. like my husband Andy. I find myself flailing in this cramped space, arms and legs churning wildly in this storm, my head jouncing above and below water. Sometimes I take refuge in the bathroom. I need somewhere to breathe in and out hard. Or the laundry room. Usually the kitchen. My laptop is set up on the counter next to half-eaten apples and sippy cups tacky from juice. I peruse all manner of social media for stories about the outside world. I come across images of crowds filling the streets in Ferguson, Mo. A different kind of commotion, and one that shifts my perspective in those brief moments.

My head snaps up as the children protest my lack of providing "fair" judgment when it comes to whose turn it is to play with the plastic, much too lifelike frog or Thomas the Tank Engine. A wailing ensues that threatens to drown the last of my brain cells, obliterating any ability to make a clear decision. I despair a little trying to imagine how I might possibly provide them with a reasonable perspective. I'm overwhelmed, for these people have reasons for making noise.

I read Mark's telling of the story of the hemorrhaging woman and Jairus' daughter and feel a bit of mental commotion. I see a provocative mingling here—an old woman with a persistent blood disease and a prepubescent girl on her deathbed. Still, both are in need of Jesus' touch, whether to touch or to be touched by a power that gives life, and not only new life but a touch that gives life back.

I ponder their bodies. The woman who was likely deemed untouchable—physically, socially and emotionally—and who was in major isolation because of the impurity of this persistent bleeding. It is unholy and unclean, and she knows it. I wonder, Where is her family? Does she have a husband or children? What would it be like to not touch them or be touched by them for 12 years? What would it be like to not have children running between her legs or entreating her to sit so they can dog-pile her for an hour even though there are plenty of seats elsewhere, for the sole purpose of being near her? What would it mean to get my life and my body back so I could feel the butterfly kisses of my children and the embrace of my husband or parents?

Jesus healed her without being conscious of it. When she touched him, he noticed something had changed in him. I am moved by the way this woman's touch moved him. I want to play with the possibility that it even transformed him. He affirms her faith, and in doing so he affirms her agency and recognizes her will toward life. And we see here a picture of Jesus, his body, his potential for miraculous connection and even conversion.

On the other hand, Jairus' family, overcome with grief, laugh derisively at Jesus when he says the little girl is not dead but only sleeping. Undaunted by their perspective, he heals her, and she gets up to walk around, shaking the sleep out of her limbs as if she were waking up for breakfast and getting ready to head off to school. I wonder if the daughter was even aware of her death, if she was confused at all by the tears of surprise and relief of her family. Did Jairus sweep the little girl up into the air? Did her mother cover her with kisses of grateful disbelief? Did she pull her daughter close, smelling her hair, feeling her breath on her face, her fingers around her neck and her warm blood pulsating beneath her skin, pumping hard from a strong heart?

My mind shifts to Ferguson and the videos of Lesley McSpadden after the grand-jury decision not to indict Darren Wilson for the murder of her son Michael Brown. I watch her body crumple to the ground. She lifts up her face to the sky, and her mouth is contorted in agony, her cheeks covered in tears. Her voice keening, she is wailing, and I can feel it reverberate across my own flesh and blood, in my skin and marrow—the loss of life and the loss of justice. I see the streets of New York City, Chicago, Detroit and even Bloomington fill up with people of all colors marching with signs that say #blacklivesmatter. The people walk together like resistance is the new air, we breathe it, and I look at my little girl Anna next to me holding her sign. Before we leave to go home for dinner and baths, we stand with the group for $4^1/_2$ minutes in silence to remember Michael Brown's body dead in the street for $4^1/_2$ hours. The red and blue lights of police cars in my eyes and cars rushing by on the other side of the street—I weep a little and breathe out, "Lord Jesus, hear our prayer."

Anna is on my back in the baby carrier. She is asleep but begins to wake up, softly crying over and over, "Mommy, Mommy, Mommy..." My heart falters at the thought of the cries of the men and women lying in the streets—someone's babies   and how they went unheard and were silenced by violence and death. I think about the strangled noises of life leaving bodies that were brutally shot or killed with bare hands. I think about mothers and fathers collapsing to the ground wailing for lost children. I think about suicide bombers and school shootings and massacres and buildings falling on top of people—lives, voices, bodies.

Why all this commotion and wailing? It feels rhetorical.

Come, Lord, Jesus, come quickly.

Mihee Kim-Kort *is an ordained minister in the Presbyterian Church (USA) and the author of* Making Paper Cranes, Streams Run Uphill *and* Yoked: Stories of a Clergy Couple in Marriage, Family, and Ministry.

RITA NAKASHIMA BROCK

"Don't you see that nothing that enters a person from the outside can defile them?"

(MARK 7:18)

---•••---

In 1993, when wars in Central America dominated the news, the National Council of Churches sent me to El Salvador and Guatemala with a small international delegation to see how churches could support U.N.-brokered agreements between the governments and revolutionary movements. We met with heads of state, military officers, human-rights groups, clergy and revolutionary leaders, the papal nuncio, U.N. officials and Nobel Peace Prize winner Rigoberta Menchú.

In Guatemala, bleak conditions for the people had developed over a decades-long civil war in which the government, aided by the U.S., inflicted a fierce "white terror" campaign against indigenous Mayans, activists, refugees, academics and students, left-leaning politicians, trade unionists, journalists and street children.

Destitute people by the thousands lived in the toxic Guatemala City dump, where families and orphaned children scavenged for basic necessities.

One evening, a Nazarene community of urban peasants hosted us for dinner. The entire community awaited our arrival and welcomed us with music and prayer. We sat with them among long rows of tables covered with white cloth and set with the most extravagant dinner they could afford: hot homemade tortillas, beans and grilled steak.

I was seated across from two young men who fidgeted awkwardly. They thanked me for visiting their church and proudly passed me a platter of steak and tortillas. I was a macrobiotic vegetarian at the time. I had a second of indecision before I realized I would feel terrible if I refused the meat. I took the smallest steak, cut a piece and began chewing ... and chewing.

As I sought a discreet way to remove the tough wad from my mouth, I glanced up and saw the young men vigorously chewing. We locked eyes and simultaneously broke out laughing. We continued to giggle as we valiantly gnawed through the feast. I received a warm hug from them when we left.

A few months later, further government instability delayed a brokered peace for several more years in Guatemala. As I watched the news and worried about the country, I thought of that meal and the two young men who had shared their hospitality with me.

When Jesus asked the question "Don't you see that nothing that enters a person from the outside can defile them?," he was commenting on a text from the prophet Isaiah, who challenged the privileged with a call for justice: "This people honors me with their lips [what they eat], but their hearts are far from me."

Our delegation was invited to dinner because we represented an international community of Christians concerned about the long, intractable civil war in Guatemala. Had I refused the steak, I would have refused food in a country where children eat garbage to survive. Privilege and its protections allow us to think that regardless of where we go and what we do, we are just individuals. Strangers, however, judge us as products of our cultures and communities in ways as subtle as noticing what our eyes do when we speak to them or how we receive a gift.

I remain ashamed that I almost refused the church's hospitality and turned myself into a guest unworthy of their hope for peace and better, safer lives. I almost failed my own deepest commitments to justice and peace.

Lately, however, I have been thinking about how simple my choice was as a guest at that meal. Much more difficult were our meetings with the country's politicians and military leaders, who maintained the white-terror campaign. I had a closed heart and assumed we would hear little that would be true or offer hope for peace.

I did not consider the choices facing a leader who protected the vested interests of the rich and powerful. What if his country's economy would collapse or his own family would be ruined or assassinated if he failed? Not once did I consider the cost to a career soldier who rose up the ranks as a peasant and who had to issue orders to shoot children, slaughter protesters and burn alive those who refused to leave their land. Nor did I consider the men who followed his orders, trapped in an unavoidable civil war.

In the dire circumstances of war, every decision may result in death or loss. Some people learn to harden their hearts and do what they feel they must. They deny that what they do violates the moral code of human society—perhaps even the moral code of the conduct of war.

A hardened heart can defile someone for a lifetime, but sometimes, the heart breaks. This breaking is the mystery of human moral conscience, its fierce spiritual power haunting us after some of the worst ways humans have designed to destroy conscience.

Whatever the hopes for a cause, those who fight are often left with grief and exhaustion, hollowed out inside. They may have nightmares and feel confused, angry or disillusioned with their cause. Faced with harrowing choices that offer only terrible or worse alternatives, survivors may come to feel guilty and ashamed for what they did or failed to do. They may decide they are no longer a good person and reject their faith in God. Moral injury is one name for that kind of broken heart.

I wonder if my dinner companions joined the resistance. Do pink mists of killing, lifeless stares, shattering bombs, decaying corpses and acrid cordite clouds haunt their dreams? If they survived to go home, they probably carried broken hearts.

The achievement of peace is a continual struggle. We must not only attend to the victims of war and violence but also examine our relationships with those who inflict violence, especially those who do so on behalf of their countries or people. If we can explore our own moral responsibility for violence done for us by others, we will be more deeply embedded in the struggle for peace, rather than setting ourselves apart from those with broken hearts.

This opening of the heart rests in the mystery of ancient wisdom that embraces repentance, recompense and restoration. It enables communities to mend broken relationships while protecting victims from further harm, to lament the profound losses that violence inflicts and to seek to enable life to flourish. Then, transformed within, whatever comes from us will not defile us.

Rita Nakashima Brock *is the founding co-director of the Soul Repair Center at Brite Divinity School in Texas.*

CARRIE NEWCOMER

"Why does this generation ask for a sign?"

(MARK 8:12)

—•••—

Albert Einstein said, "We can choose to look at the world in one of two ways—as if nothing is a miracle, or as if everything is a miracle." I know when the world feels anything less than miraculous to me, I'm probably not paying attention. The group of people Jesus was talking to in this Gospel story wanted hard evidence of the sacred presence—a flashy, parting-of-the-Red Sea verification. Jesus responded with a question, inviting them—and us—to reframe what it means to see and experience the living presence. He invited them to think of a miracle as more than a statement punctuated with a period, rather, as part of an ongoing spiritual conversation including many heart-opening questions. How and where does the sacred presence move in our daily lives and world? If I experience a sacred presence within me and all around me, how then shall I live with this knowledge?

As a spiritual songwriter, I often wonder and write about

experiencing the mysterious indwelling of the sacred—in Quakerism referred to as "that of God in everyone" or "the Light"— in ordinary things and daily experiences. Consistently, when I am open to a daily relationship with wonder, wonder usually shows up, or more likely, I finally see what has always been there. I live in southern Indiana, about where the glaciers of the last ice age stopped. It is a rolling green area with deep ravines and lovely deciduous forests. It is also the home to an unusual abundance of a particular kind of stone called the geode. On the outside, geodes look like lumpy gray-brown rocks, but inside they are filled with beautiful quartz crystals.

There is a creek that runs through the woods where I live, and it is filled with these amazing rocks. In Monroe County, Indiana, geodes are as common as corn, and yet each one is a wonder. I have a friend from New York who came out to visit me in the wilds of the Midwest. I took her for a walk thinking we would pick up a few geodes in the creek. She kept looking around, saying, "I don't see them. Where are they?" Finally I picked up one and showed it to her. I said, "See, they look like lumpy, brown brains on the outside." Then she stopped and looked around and said, "Oh my gosh, they're everywhere. They are absolutely everywhere." Now that she had seen the miracle, she could not unsee it.

All these things that we call familiar,
Are just miracles clothed in the commonplace
You'll see it if you try in the next stranger's eyes,
God walks around in muddy boots,
Sometimes rags and that's the truth,
You can't always tell, but sometimes you just know.
FROM "GEODES," BY CARRIE NEWCOMER

When I began sensing the Light in even ordinary things, it changed how I experienced the world, reframing it in a way that counteracted our cultural narrative of lack and replaced it with a wondrous sense of abundance, gratitude and responsibility. I remember taking my daughter to the Monet room at the Chicago Art Institute when she was 5. I had shown her postcards of his haystack paintings, explaining that this artist loved the way things looked and felt in different kinds of light and that he used tiny dabs of color to re-create the feelings he loved so much. When we entered the room, she stood transfixed. Then she ran up to the haystack painting and stood so close to the image, it dissolved into individual strokes. She said, "It's gone. It's just little dots." Then she walked backward until she was standing next to me, viewing the painting again as a whole. She took my hand and breathed, "There it is. I see it, and it's totally made of magic." I said, "Yes, honey, that's how it all works."

The world is made of water and dust, ordinary physical things, but all of them are filled with miracle, Light and considerable magic. When I see the world with this frame, small things take on a luminous quality and daily actions become a sacrament. There is no need to wait for a miracle as proof—the miracle we need is already here

Holy is the dish and drain,
The soap and sink, the cup and plate
And warm wool socks, and the cold white tile
Showerheads and good dry towels.
And frying eggs sound like psalms
With a bit of salt measured in my palm,
It's all a part of a sacrament,
As holy as a day is spent.

Holy is the busy street
And the cars that boom with passion's beat,
And the checkout girl, counting change,
And the hands that shook my hands today.
Hymns of geese fly overhead
And stretch their wings like their parents did
Blessed be the dog that runs in her sleep
To catch some wild and elusive thing.

Holy is a familiar room
And the quiet moments in the afternoon.
And folding sheets like folding hands,
To pray as only laundry can.
I'm letting go of all I fear,
Like autumn leaves of earth and air.
For summer came and summer went,
As holy as a day is spent.

Holy is the place I stand,
To give whatever small good I can,
And the empty page, the open book,
Redemption everywhere I look.
Unknowingly we slow our pace,
In the shade of unexpected grace,
With grateful smiles and sad lament
As holy as a day is spent.

And morning light sings "Providence"
As holy as a day is spent.

FROM "HOLY AS THE DAY IS SPENT," BY CARRIE NEWCOMER

Carrie Newcomer *is a Quaker songwriter, recording artist, performer, author and educator. She has 15 internationally released recordings and is a prominent voice for progressive spirituality and social and environmental justice.*

WALTER BRUEGGEMANN

"Why are you talking about having no bread?"

(MARK 8:17)

—·••·—

BREAD TALK

The narrative reports that Jesus fed 5,000 people and had 12 baskets of bread left over (Mark 6:30–44). Then he fed 4,000 people and had seven baskets left over (Mark 8:1–10). But even after all of that, his disciples had anxiety about bread. Their anxiety seems a misfit with the abundance of bread. In response, Jesus asks his disciples, "Why are you talking about having no bread?" (Mark 8:17). Perhaps he is astonished at their obtuseness. More likely he is irritated that they do not trust his abundance.

I.

Either way, we still talk about bread:

> It is the staff of life;
> It is the irreducible sustainer of life;
> It is the meeting place when "we break bread together."
>> It must be given, and received, broken and
>> shared, and chewed.

It may be buttered and sliced and toasted.
Life depends on it!
We still talk about having no bread, or not enough
or bread that is organic or gluten-free.

II.

The first time we talked about no bread was back with father
Abraham and mother Sarah (Genesis 12:10) ... in a famine.
We knew what to do.
We went to Egypt and we ate the bread of Pharaoh;
It turned out to be a hazardous way to secure bread.
The second time we talked about no bread was after we left
Pharaoh's Egypt (Exodus 16:2–5).
Pharaoh had plenty of bread. But we entered wilderness
where there was no bread.
We complained; Moses was irritated with us.
But God gave bread.
It came down from heaven;
We were surprised and did not recognize it.
We said, "What is it *(man-hu)*? And it was named
"manna."
We wondered about it; it turned out to be
Wonder Bread sent from heaven above.
There was enough for all; each one took what was needed.
But we could not store up any surplus.
Provision was made for Sabbath rest; we had no
need to gather bread on Sabbath ... real rest!!
But then "manna ceased" (Joshua 5:12).
We knew bread from heaven,
but now bread from the earth, by soil and labor and

agriculture
> and plowing and planting and harvesting and
> storing.
Our bread became quarrelsome,
> because some had big granaries
> and some had nothing;
> children starved, and
>   men fought over bread, and
> mothers cried about the lack for their children.
Later on the poet chided us (Isaiah 55:1–2),
> because we had signed on for bread from the empire,
> from the military, from the banks, from the greed system.
The poet wondered why we labored for such bread
>   that did not satisfy or nourish;
> we engaged in endless work and hopeless
> productivity,
> and we remained hungry for real bread instead
> of such pretend bread.
But the poet offered otherwise: "free bread, free water,
free milk,"
> all gifts, "sent from heaven above."

III.

Our mouths and our bodies are filled with bread talk,
> Of Pharaoh's bread,
> Of bread from heaven,
> Of bread from the earth via what,
> Of bread that does not satisfy,
> Of bread that is free ... and abundant!

IV.

Then he came. His mother had anticipated:
>   she anticipated what God would do ...
>>   fill the hungry with good things, and
>>   send the rich empty away (Luke 1:53).

She expected the redistribution of bread
>   that would change the world
>>   and all its social relationships.
>   He came, he taught, he fed, he healed,
>>   he surprised, he transformed.

And finally he took bread;
>   He said, "This is my body."
>   We have argued and wondered what he meant by that.
>   But we Christians in the meantime
>>   keep receiving his awesome bread.
>>   We chew and sometimes we receive news with
>>   the bread.
>>>   We are fed!

V.

From that table of welcome,
>   we dare imagine "Bread for the World."
>   We dare to assert that "Loaves abound!"
>   We imagine and assert right in the midst of hungry social
>   reality.

We know very well
>   that bread is managed by the rich and the powerful,
>   that force of arms assures an unequal supply of bread,
>   that greed denies others enough bread to live,

that the earth from which comes bread is being choked
off in greed and chemicals,
that debt cuts people off from the bread supply,
that greed and scarcity,
self-indulgence and poverty go together
bonded by cheap labor.
We know this! We see this all around! We do not blink before it ...
except in shame.

VI.

And then, knowing and seeing and blinking in shame,
we still dare anticipatory obedience,
because bread is provided,
because bread is given.
We anticipate that God-given bread will override
all the anxious ideologies of scarcity and greed.
We still, like ancient disciples, talk of "no bread,"
and then abundance wells up in our midst,
right before our eyes,
in neighborliness,
in generosity,
in hospitality,
in valorizing "the least" among us,
right before our eyes in many forms
from charity and kindness and soup kitchens,
to policy and Marshall Plans of sustenance,
of food stamps, and debt cancellation, and living wage.
Pharaoh taught us so well about scarcity while he had surplus,
and we are in the process of unlearning the compelling
lessons of Pharaoh.

Pharaoh, it turns out,
          is contradicted by gospel abundance,
on offer in the generosity of heaven,
on offer in the "amber waves of grain" on earth,
on offer at the table where all are welcome.
As the apostle queried us:
          "What do you have that you did not receive?
          (I Corinthians 4:7).
We know the answer: "Nothing." Because all is given, more than
enough!

Walter Brueggemann *is a professor emeritus of the Old Testament at*
Columbia Theological Seminary in Georgia and the author of many books.

CHRISTIAN WIMAN

"Who do people say I am?"

(MARK 8:27)

Jesus' question is general, social, a finger on the pulse of the people, the blab of the pave, as Walt Whitman puts it. You get the sense—I get the sense—Jesus doesn't quite care. His eyes are elsewhere, skyward.

His next question is sharp, singular, unsparing. You can imagine it cutting poor Peter to the quick. You can almost see Christ—for that's who he suddenly and searingly is—lowering his dark eyes to Peter's. Or, if you call yourself a Christian, you can feel those eyes finding that soft rot of doubt at the center of yourself. *Who do you say I am?*

When I was a child growing up in the mental prisons and wild charisms of West Texas, this crisis of consciousness, this one moment of existential decision, had a tremendous and eternal urgency. Into even the darkest hearts, it was believed, Christ turned those eyes and asked that question. Into even the darkest hearts, there came a chance—maybe just one chance—at everlasting light.

The tough thing, though, was that it didn't exactly matter

what came out of your mouth. It was a closed universe, that town, and everyone said exactly what Peter did—"You are the Christ"—whether or not they believed it in their hearts.

So that's where the preacher probed on Sundays, saying it was a question that every one of us had to answer for ourselves, or not even for ourselves, since we could deceive ourselves, but for God—who, it seemed, turned his searchlight most intensely into the recesses of those whose imaginations far outstripped their experience. Night after night I lay on the knife edge between heaven and hell while the question grew so savage and demanding and relentless that it wasn't a question at all: Who do you say I am!

In all three of the synoptic Gospels, Peter answers immediately. In all three of the synoptic Gospels (and also in John, where this question does not appear), Peter ends up denying not only that he is a follower of Christ but even that he knows the man at all. The strange thing—and maybe the saving thing—is that Jesus himself predicts this.

In the tradition of biblical literalism in which I grew up, there was one sin so egregious, so hell-foul and final, that even God could not forgive it. You could not slander the Holy Ghost. Worse than furtive sex at the Sonic, worse than murder, worse, apparently, than the impulses behind the Holocaust and Hiroshima—there was this one betrayal, which might be entirely private.

Of course telling this to a child is like the old game in which you tell him "Don't think of a polar bear," and I still remember—still viscerally feel—lying in bed trying with all my might not to slander the Holy Ghost until finally my tongue was touched with an altogether unholy fire: "F--- the Holy Ghost!" I whispered into my Tarzan sheets, bracing myself for the onslaught.

The Holy Ghost is the spirit of Christ left behind for humans after Christ ascends to heaven. The worst has happened: God is dead. The best has happened: He is risen. But now, because of some theological logic that theologians have never quite untied, Christ must ascend to heaven and leave us limping once more toward what feels, especially in modern times, suspiciously similar to oblivion. Our consolation prize is the Holy Ghost, which is Jesus' presence in our hearts, which is sometimes—a latter slander?—damnably inadequate. Who do you say I am? A ghost.

When my great-grandmother died in 1991 at the age of 95, I was living on the outskirts of Prague. I went for a long walk in a forested area near my apartment trying to feel something appropriate to the occasion. I spent a lot of time back then doing that. Trying to feel, I mean.

Everything was white: the birch trees, the fog, the sky, my mind. I thought of my great-grandmother being married away at 14 and hiding under the bed from her hatchet-faced husband; and of the mythic months she spent mute and prone after losing too many people she had loved; and of her making her aching way to the back door, saying, "I guess the good Lord don't give us more than we can bear," bearing a tub of candied yams or crushed squash to some family dinner that seemed fraught with finality long before it actually was—when suddenly a branch right above me turned into a huge albino bird that I could not identify.

It was the closest thing to a vision that I have ever had, and I wanted—I needed—to know what that bird was. But every time I drew near, it took off again into the whiteness, until finally, with huge otherworldly wings, it cleared the last line of trees and ghosted the mist over the river, escaping any name I might have given it.

The power of the word of God comes not from its solidity, not from its being hammered into stones with which to beat the heads of humans. No, the power of the word of God, just like the power of poetry, comes precisely from its mercurial meanings, its tendency to slide free of every attempt to pin it down and to insinuate itself into every single life in a different way.

My great-grandmother read the Bible through every year of her adult life. It was, so far as I know, the only book she ever read. Out of the mouth of God, filtered through Hebrew and Greek and Latin, forged by wars and committees and blood feuds so fierce that even monks became butchers over the question of Jesus' divinity—down, down, down into a little trailer in Texas, there trickles the King's English ("But whom say ye that I am") for one old woman to ponder and puzzle over and worketh out her own salvation in fear and trembling. There is something absurd and hopeless about such an effort, to be sure. And heroic. Forget the theologians and the scholars, forget the preachers and the poets: Who do you, Mamie Thrailkill, in your heart of hearts, say I am?

How much of life is living up to a call we're never quite sure we heard? Peter's answer is the one that Scripture has him giving immediately—"You are the Christ"—and it is also his adamant denial of Jesus in Jerusalem. It is the church founded on Peter's name, and it is the immutable muteness that lies within every authoritative statement that every church attempts to make. The truth and the lie. The rock and the rot. There is no answer to Jesus' question, and yet you must wager everything upon it.

Christian Wiman *is the author of numerous books. He teaches at the Yale Institute of Sacred Music.*

MARK BURNETT

"How long has he been like this?"

(MARK 9:21)

My son Cameron dedicated the entire summer before his senior year of high school to taking on endless hours of AP classes in order to finish earlier to be free to work on our NBC production *A.D.: The Bible Continues.* He intends to study film in college, so it made sense, and in late August we packed our bags and headed across the world to southern Morocco for months of filming.

We got settled in Ouarzazate, a beautiful oasis town where Ridley Scott made the movies *Gladiator* and *Kingdom of Heaven* and where my wife Roma Downey and I filmed our highly successful miniseries *The Bible* in 2012. It's an amazing, exotic location that conjures up images of ancient times and was perfect for *A.D.*

We were full of excitement and anticipation, but things took an awful turn. Cameron fell ill, and while we initially blamed his illness on a stomach bug, it became apparent that this was something much more serious. Within 10 days we were on a medical jet heading across the Atlantic and back to the U.S. to get him surgical treatment for a neuroendocrine tumor in his head.

It was an 18-hour flight between stops, but we managed to safely transport Cameron home. I was relieved to be back, and we rushed him to a hospital, where he underwent a 10-hour surgery that proved to be successful. However, just as we thought we were out of the woods, Cameron encountered serious complications that were worse than the original condition and the surgery. He was left unable to speak or control his limbs. What we would end up experiencing during the next few weeks can only be described as a living nightmare for Cameron and a parent's worst fear.

The doctors weren't sure that Cameron would ever fully recover, and I was left feeling helpless. They explained that his speech would be the last thing to return and that it could take months. Although he desperately wanted to communicate, he was essentially locked in. It was awful for him. As a parent, you feel that you are supposed to be able to fix everything for your child, but this was a situation that I had no control over. It was absolutely heartbreaking. I wanted so much to take away the fear and pain he was experiencing, so I did the only thing I knew how to do: I put all of my faith in prayer.

I prayed as hard as I could, and as a family we reached out to prayer groups worldwide. Cameron's eyes seemed to beg me daily to understand what he wanted to communicate. It was excruciating. I questioned multiple doctors, but none could give me a clear answer. In fact, they seemed nervous. They had never seen this complication before. These were my darkest days.

I only had my faith. In the moments when Cameron slept, I tried to read my Bible, but it was hard to focus. Then one night I found myself staring at the Book of Mark, specifically the story in the ninth chapter about the child who was unable to speak. Despite their trying, disciples had failed to cure him. Jesus asks the boy's father, "How long has he been like this?" The boy's father replies, "From childhood"—this father had faced fear for his son far longer than I had. Jesus then intervened, and immediately the boy was able to speak. The disciples were confused. In the past, they, too, had cured illnesses, but Jesus explained that in a case like this only prayer worked.

I knew it was a sign—I just knew it. I prayed harder, I focused on that Scripture and I asked Jesus to do for Cameron what he had done for that boy. My faith is strong, and I felt I had been guided to that text. Jesus was going to perform a miracle on Cameron. I prayed even harder in the following days.

Then one afternoon Cameron motioned for me to come closer, and I heard his weak but understandable first words: "I'm thirsty." I was so overwhelmed, I just stared at him. Then I hugged him. His voice repeated, "I'm thirsty," and I grabbed water for him and watched him sip. He had spoken. Our prayers were answered. I read that Scripture over and over, and I know I was directed to it. He had defied the medical prognosis. The doctors were partially amazed and completely relieved. The prayer groups increased their efforts and the miracles continued.

Over the next few days, Cameron's speech returned. Then, amazingly and in defiance of medical conventional wisdom, a boy who was going through complications so rare that hardly any doctors had ever dealt with them—and who was expected to recover at the earliest over the course of many months—got up one day and walked two steps. Days after that he walked his way around the entire hospital ward. Within weeks he resumed driving, and today he's back on the set of one of our TV shows.

As Paul writes in the New Testament Book of Romans, prayer

will always provide hope: "Remember that suffering produces perseverance; perseverance, character; and character, hope."

Mark Burnett *is the CEO of United Artists Media Group in Los Angeles. He is the producer of* Survivor, The Voice, Shark Tank, The Apprentice, Are You Smarter Than a 5th Grader? *and, with wife Roma Downey, the producer of* The Bible, *its sequel* A.D.: The Bible Continues *and* Ben-Hur.

BARRY C. BLACK

"How can you make it salty again?"

(MARK 9:50)

—•••—

Like any capable attorney, Jesus asked questions whose answers he already knew. In Mark 9:50 he asked a question that he answered in Matthew 5:13: "You are the salt of the earth; but if salt has lost its taste how shall its saltiness be restored?" He then provided this answer: "It is no longer good for anything except to be thrown out and trodden underfoot by people." Jesus essentially said that taste-less salt is useless.

Why did Jesus ask this question about tasteless salt? He was speaking to a multitude on a mountain, but more particularly to his 12 disciples. Perhaps he wanted his hearers to comprehend that they could be an influence for good or evil. They could leave a corrupt and dark world better or worse than they found it. Like salt, their influence had antiseptic powers, bringing purity to a polluted world. Like salt, their influence had vivifying powers, bringing flavor to an insipid world. And like salt, their influence had preservative powers, holding at bay putrefaction and decay in a rotting world.

Notice what Jesus expected regarding the breadth of their

outreach. The disciples weren't just salt for the community, state or nation but for the earth, an influence with a potentially global impact. Perhaps this is why his final marching order to them in his Great Commission (Matthew 28:19) was: "Go into all the world and make disciples, baptizing them in the name of the Father, Son, and Holy Spirit." He spoke a similar sentiment in Acts 1:8: "You will be my witnesses in Jerusalem, Judea, Samaria, and to the uttermost parts of the earth." He may have wanted them to know that when they abused their God-given influence, the consequences wouldn't just be local.

Perhaps Jesus spoke of tasteless salt because he wanted his followers to make their influence felt through exemplary living, bringing purifying power to their world. He may have wanted them to embrace the behavior later advocated in Colossians 4:6: "Let your speech be always with grace, seasoned with salt, that ye may know how ye ought to answer everyone." He urged that they speak this way in Matthew 5:44: "Bless those who curse you and pray for those who despitefully use you." Martin Luther King Jr. talked about what can happen when we fail to make our influence matter. He said, "History will have to record that the greatest tragedy of this period of social transition was not the strident clamor of the bad people, but the appalling silence of the good people." God expects more than tasteless silence from his followers. He wants them to be "living letters from Christ" (2 Corinthians 3:3).

Perhaps Jesus asked this question to emphasize that misused influence perpetuates corruption in our world. He may have wanted his disciples to appreciate the fact that their mission was to arrest the stench of decay and bring life and health. G. Campbell Morgan, the great British preacher of the early 20th century, put it this way: "Jesus, looking out over the multitudes of his day, saw the corruption, the disintegration of life at every point, its breakup, its spoliation; and, because of His love of the multitudes, He knew the thing that they needed most was salt in order that the corruption could be arrested."

Perhaps Jesus asked this question about tasteless salt to show his disciples that misused influence takes flavor out of our world. Biblical commentator Matthew Henry said: "Mankind, living in ignorance and wickedness, were like a rubbish heap, ready to rot; but Christ sent forth his disciples, whose lives and doctrines could season the earth with knowledge and grace. If they are not what they should be, they are like salt that has lost its savor." Elihu Buritt explains it another way: "No human being can come into this world without increasing or decreasing the sum total of human happiness, not only of the present but of every subsequent age of humanity." When people of faith misuse their influence, they decrease the sum of human happiness, making their world less palatable.

What a blessing to be useful salt that purifies, flavors and preserves. U.S. President Woodrow Wilson once talked about an experience he had at a barbershop. A man came in and sat in the barber's chair next to him and showed such a personal interest in the man cutting his hair that the atmosphere in the room changed. "I was aware I had attended an evangelistic service, because Mr. D.L. Moody was in that chair," Wilson later reflected. "They did not know his name, but they knew something had elevated their thoughts, and I felt that I left that place as I should have left a place of worship." Moody became salt to everyone in that room.

Like a good attorney, Jesus knew the answer to the question he asked about tasteless salt; it is useless. Could he, therefore, be saying to people of faith today, "Followers of mine, cultivate useful influence; bring purity, flavor and preservation to life"? Use your savory influence to quicken the conscience of the wayward, elevate the conversation of the cynical and restrain the corruption of the deviant. Serve my purpose for your life by making an antiseptic, vivifying and preservative impact on your world. Could he be challenging people of faith to permit their powerful influence to make the world thirstier for the waters of life?

Barry C. Black *is the chaplain of the U.S. Senate.*

MARILYNNE ROBINSON

"Why do you call me good?"

(MARK 10:18)

—•••—

In the course of his brief ministry, Jesus often scandalized the righteous and offended the religious. So when a man of sincere and scrupulous conventional piety calls him good, he might reasonably wonder what the man sees in him. I assume the stranger wears the attire, the fringes and earlocks, that would signify to Jesus his strict obedience to the laws of Moses. He not only kneels to Jesus but asks him for guidance in the matter to which his piety is addressed, and for which it seems to him inadequate. He asks Jesus what he can do to inherit eternal life. Jesus refers him to the Ten Commandments, exactly the moral regime the man has followed from his youth and that has left him uncertain. So Jesus tells him to sell all he has, give the money to the poor and follow him. The man, who is very rich, goes away sorrowing, his desire for eternal life apparently less compelling than his attachment to his wealth.

We are told that Jesus loves this man, this stranger with his urgent question. Their encounter would seem to be a perfect opportunity for him to declare, as he does elsewhere, "Woe to you rich!" Indeed, he does liken the entry of a rich man into heaven to a camel passing through the eye of a needle. And then he says, in effect, God does not pause over such impossibilities. God would love this man, too, and no more condemn him than Jesus does. It seems that Jesus sees goodness in him which does not consist in his piety and is not diminished by his fault. Then the encounter becomes a small parable about the freedom of God and the mystery of grace.

How is Jesus' question, his querying the word *good,* part of the story as it occurs in Matthew, Mark and Luke? Why is the story always the context of the question, its gloss? Scholars often attribute these recurrences in the synoptic Gospels to a source text that passed among their writers, perhaps the Gospel of Mark itself. Whatever their origin, the fact that they are preserved in every telling means that they are valued moments in the tradition of Jesus that the Gospels reflect, that they are rich in implication.

Jewish piety always insisted on the unique goodness of God. So, with his question, Jesus is correcting this very pious man toward purer orthodoxy, perhaps smiling as he does so. He is placing himself within the world of Jewish faith, as he also does when he says, in response to the man's question, "You know the commandments." That is to say, the commandments are sufficient to your need.

It is strange that we know Jewish Jesus through Greek, a language he presumably did not speak. The Septuagint, a body of pre-Christian translations of the Hebrew Bible into Greek, had a great influence on Jewish thought and on the New Testament particularly. Biblical Greek reflects distinctions not available in Hebrew, Latin or English. Hebrew *tov,* good, is translated into Greek by various words with interesting differences of meaning.

The Greek words are in turn translated into Latin by the one word *bonus* and into English by the one word *good*—a good tree (*agathos*) brings forth good fruit (*kalos*). Generalization is unwise, but *agathos* suggests a primary and essential goodness, *kalos* a very real but derived goodness—light and all the stages of creation are *kalos* in the Septuagint. The rich man greets Jesus with the first of these words when he calls him "good teacher," and this may be what Jesus objects to, honoring a Jewish scruple that the Greek language makes clear and English obscures. In any case, Jesus is insisting here on his own creatureliness, which is full of meaning at this point in the Gospel, when he is turning toward Jerusalem and toward his own very human suffering and death.

Perhaps the conservatism of the Gospels in preserving moments like this one is a response to their raising questions they do not resolve. If the commandments are sufficient for eternal life, what is or was the mission of Jesus? What is the point of offering a morally charged metaphor for the impossible and then saying that with God nothing is impossible? Why refuse negative judgment of a man who has walked away from Jesus' offer to accept him as a follower? Why reject the stranger's acknowledgment of the highest order of goodness in him, which might, to the man's credit, reflect an intuition that Jesus is much more than a teacher? Every question is live, and none of them is trivial. One of these writers might have changed the story so that Jesus welcomed the honor of the man's greeting, proposed himself as the answer to the man's uncertainty, then condemned his materialism and his rejection of the offer of salvation. It would seemingly amount to little more than reconciling a few details to a broader narrative.

But the Gospels are first of all records of an extraordinary presence. The disciples tend to be more or less confounded by what they see and hear, and their bewilderment is also recorded. It is perfectly appropriate to imagine them, when the rich man had gone away, asking one another what had just happened, why that small encounter was so pleasing and so unsettling. Their faithfulness to their experience and to the strange authority of Jesus would take the form of preserving anomalies like these.

Why do you call me good? The answer might have been that the rich man's sense of the divine made him restless even with the great and rigorous goodness he had embraced. Culture and language may exclude us from a full sense of what we are being told—every one of these ancient words for *good* also means beautiful. Beautiful teacher. As Jesus' destiny presses in on him, the dying man can be as free and gracious as the living God.

Marilynne Robinson *is a Pulitzer Prize–winning author and professor of English and creative writing at the University of Iowa's Writers' Workshop.*

SCOTT CAIRNS

"Can you drink the cup I drink or be baptized with the baptism I am baptized with?"

—•••—

As with many disconcerting
                puzzles, as with most
questions one may first be slow
                or too embarrassed to answer,
his provocations can educe
                a glib array of other
questions, most of which
                are offered mostly to defer,
evade or qualify one's
                shamed reluctance to say yes.

Which cup, Lord? What baptism?

Who am I to say?
In any case, I daresay Jesus
                is not speaking of the cup
at Canna, nor of that cup
                he asked of Photini;
neither—I'm guessing—
                does he indicate so much
the cup he offered his disciples
                on the night he was betrayed.

The *cup* that he himself
                would have forgone
—had it served
                the Father's will—is far
more likely the bitter
                vessel implicated here.

Nor is his humble dipping
                in the Jordan   so brief
a descent—likely to be
                the *baptism* posed before
two suddenly bold disciples,
                both of whom would
one day—even so—drink,
                descend and be interred.

In one of *his* most curious

locutions, St. Paul
writes that he rejoices
being called to offer up
with *his own body*
his share in *what*
is lacking—υστερήματα—
in the sufferings of Christ,
that he is pleased
to undertake whatever yet
is to be done.

And what of us, languishing just
here in a swoon amid
the puzzlements? What *is*
left waiting to be done?
I would suppose that we
must surely drink, descend and drown.

Scott Cairns *is a poet and professor of modern and contemporary American literature and creative writing at the University of Missouri.*

GENE ROBINSON

"What do you want me to do for you?"

(MARK 10:51)

—•••—

Jesus, known for his probing questions, asks a zinger here! For all our whining and complaining about not having what we want, humans are quite inept at knowing what we *really* want. And Jesus knows that asking this question tells him a lot about the state of a person's soul and well-being.

Usually when we ask God, or someone else, for help, we are most often asking for some perceived cause of our unhappiness to be resolved. However, there is almost always some real and profound need for which that cause is but a symptom of a deeper unhappiness. When a CEO asks for a new yacht, the real need is for a cure to the boredom experienced by a man who has everything. When people look for sex, what they really need is intimacy, a void that can never be filled by physical sex alone.

But allowing myself to acknowledge what I really need, instead of trying to get the thing that will temporarily assuage my pain, requires courage and an openness to discovering what is the true source of my anxiety and neediness. And that is a frightening proposition. Coming face to face with what I really need results in facing up to decisions I might need to make, and behaviors I might need to change, in order to be happy and free. Frankly, it's just easier to buy the latest iPhone or take another vacation or find a new sexual partner in hopes of momentarily keeping the anxiety and unhappiness at bay—or at least distracting us from doing the hard work of figuring out what we really want.

In the first book of the *Harry Potter* series, Harry finds himself in one of the Hogwarts castle's many mysterious rooms. In it, he sees a large, ornate mirror. When he peers into the looking glass, he miraculously sees his parents, who appear to stand behind him and also gaze into the mirror. Harry is an orphan and deeply misses his parents, who were killed fighting against the evil Voldemort when Harry was young. He runs to get his friend Ron and brings him to the secret room and its magical mirror, wanting to "introduce" Ron to his parents. But when Ron looks into the mirror, Ron sees himself being carried on the shoulders of his soccer teammates and celebrated as the one who won the game. Perplexed, they both go to their mentor and teacher Dumbledore, who explains that this is a very magical mirror whose special property is to reflect back to the one who looks into it "their true heart's desire." Harry has always felt alone in the world, without a family, without the continuing love of his parents. Ron has always felt unacknowledged and undervalued by his peers. And so when they look into the mirror, each sees what he most wants in the world.

Sometimes when Jesus asks what someone wants, he not only gives them what they ask for but what they need as well. On several occasions, he heals them of a particular malady (the easier part, he tells onlookers) but then proceeds to forgive them all their sins as well. He seems to know that we usually ask for the thing we think we want, believing it will make us happy and whole. But he understands that beneath the request for healing is a request that is deeper, often unspoken and even unknown to the one asking: a healing of the soul that offers the only true hope of happiness and wholeness.

Jesus' question is profound because he is listening to the asker's heart, not to his words. In this quoted passage from Mark's Gospel, "blind Bartimaeus" may be asking to receive his sight again. But Jesus knows that it is not Bartimaeus' blindness that is killing him but everyone else's condemnation of him *because* he is blind. After all, blindness, illness and other conditions of suffering were seen at the time as evidence of one's sin, or that of the person's forebears. And that meant that this blind beggar was being treated by the society that surrounded him as someone who was getting what he deserved. What Bartimaeus really wants and needs is to be treated like the child of God he is.

Jesus is also rather predictable in his choosing those of lowly means and stations in life in whom to work these miracles. Why? Because their neediness makes them fertile ground for God's grace. The high and mighty (of 1st century Palestine or of our own time!) tend to think that they are responsible for their own prosperity and good fortune, with little willingness either to acknowledge their underlying neediness or to accept any help from God or their neighbors. And so Jesus uses the outcast and marginalized to manifest God's goodness and glory.

This question, put to a blind beggar along the road to Jericho some 2,000 years ago, is one we need to ask ourselves—if we dare. What do I want? If I am praying to God, what am I asking for? Am I living my life in a way that seeks to identify and secure what would make me truly happy and whole? Or am I merely and mindlessly running from one new gadget to another exotic trip to

another relationship in an effort to distract myself from what I
• really want and need to make my life meaningful?

What if you had Harry's magic mirror? Would you have the
courage to look into it? And what do you think you would see
reflected there? What is *your* "true heart's desire"? Or as Jesus
might say, What would you like for me to do for you?

Gene Robinson *is a senior fellow at the Center for American Progress in
Washington and the recently retired IX Episcopal Bishop of New Hampshire.*

PAUL ELIE

"John's baptism— was it from heaven, or of human origin?"

(MARK 11:30)

—•••—

You know, I've never thought about it—not that I recall, anyhow.

You might think that as a writer on matters of belief, a Catholic halfway down the road of life, I would know the Gospels inside and out. I am in a committed, long-term relationship with this set of texts. I ought to know them by now, right?

Not so—not for me, and not for many. Most of us know that there's all sorts of stuff in the Gospels that has escaped our notice. And then we come upon a passage like this one, and we feel we're coming upon it for the first time.

That's how it is with the Gospels, and with Christianity generally. It's at once succinct and inexhaustible. This religion is like a rocky promontory in the part of the world where I live—a cliff face at once tumbledown and unmistakably alive. I live at the foot of the cliff. I go up when I can. I take a trail up the far side, a day hiker of the divine.

After half a life, I feel that I know this rock face. I grew up with it. I live alongside it, in its shadow. When people come from elsewhere, I speak of it as mine.

But I don't know it fully and wouldn't want to. I'll never go straight up the face, free-climbing or ascending with ropes and pulleys. That is for the true believers. And I'll never walk all the trails up the far side. I'll know some trails well and others not at all.

It means there will always be a part of the cliff I haven't gone up before. It means that going up is an ungoverned experience, an encounter rather than a personal test.

That's how I feel when I come upon this question from Mark. It's a question I've never thought about—a way up that I haven't taken before.

But of course I *have*. Because the question "John's baptism—was it from heaven, or of human origin?" is *the* religious question in our place and time. Like the cliff where I live, it is always peripherally in sight.

It's the question about contested practices such as the ordination of women and same-sex marriage and about institutions like missions and the papacy. It's the "historical-critical" question about the authority of Scripture, which bears on all the other questions, as a river runs through it.

And it's the question about Christianity itself. Of divine origin, or "just" human? Created through a touch from the divine, or a surface irregularity produced by heat and light, water and fire?

The question I thought I'd never given any thought is in fact the question I give the most thought. And it's a question that Jesus himself asked.

Which means that his questions are ours, and vice versa.

*One thing have I asked of the Lord, that I will seek after/ that I may dwell
in the house of the Lord all the days of my life/ to behold the beauty of the
Lord, and to inquire in his temple.*

That's from Psalm 27, a text Jesus in all likelihood knew well. And
that's what he is doing: inquiring in the temple.

That Jesus himself inquired in the temple should embolden
us to do so ourselves. That he asked the question of questions—
divine, or of human origin?—suggests a religious self-awareness far
beyond what Christian belief is usually given credit for.

Here's the figure about whom people in the temple for the next
20 centuries will inquire, "From heaven, or of human origin?"
Here's that figure in the temple posing the question himself.

Scholars observe that Jesus poses the question as a conundrum
for the temple experts. But what strikes me about the question is
that it has to do with a baptism. That is apt, because baptism,
down the line, is what will set Jesus' followers apart from their
Jewish brethren. And it's apt because baptism is the Christian
act in which the human is first marked as touched and sourced
by the divine

In my own experience—at the base of the cliff where I am
sitting now, writing this—questions such as this one are framed
best by artists. And it happens that two great artists of Christian belief in our place and time have dramatized the question of
Christianity's origin through attention to baptism.

Flannery O'Connor did it in her second novel, *The Violent Bear It
Away,* which involves an old man's struggle to baptize his grandson
and so rescue him from a worldly relative. O'Connor explained,
"When I write a novel in which the central action is a baptism, I
am very well aware that for a majority of my readers, baptism is a

meaningless rite, and so in my novel I have to see that this baptism carries enough awe and mystery to jar the reader into some kind of emotional recognition of its significance ... I have to make the reader feel, in his bones if nowhere else, that something is going on here that counts."

Marilynne Robinson did it with *Gilead* and its successors. In *Gilead,* the Rev. Ames, baptizing the infant son of his fellow minister the Rev. Boughton, is taken by surprise when Boughton names the boy after Ames. And Ames, recognizing a kindred soul in a woman who shows up at his church, baptizes and then marries her. Later, this woman, Lila—convinced of her unworthiness—tries to wash off her baptism as if to establish that it was human and not divine.

Twenty centuries and change later, Jesus' question is still our question. That to me suggests, if only slightly, that the question itself—from heaven, or of human origin?—is touched by the divine.

And that's enough to send me up a trail on the far side another time.

Paul Elie, *author of* The Life You Save May Be Your Own *and* Reinventing Bach, *is a senior fellow with Georgetown University's Berkley Center for Religion, Peace and World Affairs.*

EUGENE PETERSON

"Haven't you read this passage of Scripture?"

(MARK 12:10)

—•••—

This question that Jesus asks introduces a quotation from an ancient Jewish Scripture, Psalm 118:22–23:

> *The stone that the builders rejected has become head of the corner; this was the Lord's doing and it is amazing in our eyes.*

Jesus asks his hearers to look carefully at this Scripture that they all know as well as their own name—"Have you not read this?"— implying, Certainly you must have read this.

But there is a contemporary backstory to this question too: Jesus knows that his community is trying to understand who he is.

Leading up to this moment, halfway into St. Mark's Gospel (Mark 8:27–30), Jesus gathers his 12 disciples in a kind of out-of-the-way retreat in the far north of Galilee in Caesarea Philippi, away from crowds or curiosity seekers, where they will not be bothered or even recognized. He asks them what people are saying about him. The answers come back: John the Baptist [who had been beheaded], others Elijah, still others one of the prophets. And then he asks, "And you, who do you say that I am?" Peter answers, "You are the Christ." Jesus orders them not to breathe a word of it to anyone.

Immediately, Jesus starts preparing his followers for what is to come—rejection, suffering and finally death, to be followed later by the Resurrection. But Peter doesn't like what he hears and begins to rebuke Jesus for even thinking about such a thing. And Jesus in turn rebukes Peter: "Get behind me, Satan."

They then leave their retreat in Galilee and begin the long walk to the annual Passover feast in Jerusalem, a two-, maybe three-week trek. During their time on the road, Jesus tells them that when they get to Jerusalem he will be killed. He repeats the message three times on their way.

When they arrive in Jerusalem, preparations for Passover are in full swing and the bankers in the temple are exchanging foreign currencies at inflated exchange rates from the pilgrims for temple shekels in order to purchase sacrificial lambs and pigeons for the Passover feast. When Jesus sees what is happening, he gets angry at the desecration of the holy place, in Jeremiah's words turning "my house of prayer" into a "den of thieves," and he chases the bankers from the premises. This angers the priests and scribes, and they begin to look for a way to kill him. With hostility gathering around him, Jesus tells a story, a parable, to the people on the temple floor.

He tells a story about a man who plants a vineyard and when the harvest is ready sends a slave to collect the profits. The tenants beat him up. A second slave is sent and gets the same treatment, only worse. A third slave is sent and they kill him. Finally, the owner sends his son thinking they would never kill his son. He is wrong—they not only kill him but desecrate his body.

This story concludes with Jesus' question, a nonthreatening question with not a hint of hostility, "Haven't you read this passage of Scripture: 'The stone the builders rejected has become the cornerstone; the Lord has done this, and it is marvelous in our eyes'?"

Then, after Jesus finished, the religious opposition "realized that he had told the parable against them." A growing enmity to Jesus flared—Jesus' death was as good as accomplished. Given the circumstances, it is an amazingly mild, courteous question asking them to pay attention to what they are doing—getting rid of the cornerstone.

Jesus, the Word made Flesh, is the defining revelation of God among us. This question, like all of Jesus' questions, is an invitation for us to participate in his stories. The Christian life has often suffered the indignity among many of being treated as a desiccated verbal artifact poked and probed by arthritic octogenarians of the sort skewered by poet Robert Browning as "dead from the waist down" or by "tenants" in God's vineyard who want grapes without God. The stories of Scripture provide a dependable feet-on-the-ground orientation for living this God-created life.

It is a question to remind us of the Scripture, full of stories of faith, that comes before us and speaks into stories of our own day. Without the questions, we could easily end up as spectators to who God is and what he is doing. Without the stories, we would be in danger of inhabiting a depersonalized so-called existence without substance. The life we have given to us must not be depersonalized into information about God. And it must not be functionalized into a program of strategic planning for God. When our lives are either depersonalized or functionalized, relationality diminishes and life leaks out.

Jesus asks the questions that bring us into personal participation in his work of bringing us life, life and more life.

Eugene Peterson *is a professor emeritus of spiritual theology at Regent College in British Columbia, Canada, and the author of* The Message: The Bible in Contemporary Language.

KWOK PUI-LAN

"Whose image is this? And whose inscription?"

(MARK 12:16)

—•••—

I grew up in the former British colony of Hong Kong. Our coins used to bear the image of the head of the British monarch wearing her crown, with the inscription QUEEN ELIZABETH THE SECOND in English. The coins conveyed imperial authority and the British Empire's wealth and power. The return of Hong Kong to China in 1997 necessitated the issuing of new coins, with the purple bauhinia, the city's flower, replacing the image of the Queen.

In Jesus' time, Roman coins were tangible representations of imperial power and instruments of political propaganda, glorifying the deeds of the emperor. The Roman Emperor Tiberius ruled over a vast territory, including Palestine. The Tiberius denarius was minted in silver, bearing the Caesar's image, crowned with the laurels of victory and divinity. Circumscribed around the image was an abbreviation in Latin, which can be translated as "Tiberius Caesar, Worshipful Son of the God, Augustus."

After Jesus entered Jerusalem, he cleansed the temple by chasing away those selling and buying there and turning over the tables of the money changers. His actions and parables provoked the priests, scribes and elders who questioned where his authority came from. Some Pharisees and Herodians wanted to get rid of him and so came to entrap him. They asked, "Is it right to pay the imperial tax to Caesar or not?" This tax the Pharisees asked about was the poll tax levied by the Romans on every adult listed in the census, and it could be paid in silver denarius. The colonized Jewish people hated the Roman taxes and rose up in decades-long tax revolts and other forms of resistance, culminating in the eruption of warfare in 66 C.E.

So Jesus was caught in a catch-22 situation. If he were to reply that they should pay the Roman tax, he risked angering the crowd, who would rise up against him. If he were to reply they should not pay the tax, the Pharisees could find an excuse to bring accusations against him.

Jesus correctly recognized the Pharisees' hypocrisy and did not reply directly. Instead, he asked them to bring him a denarius and posed a counter question, "Whose image is this? And whose inscription?" To which they replied, "Caesar's." Jesus then said, "Give back to Caesar what is Caesar's and to God what is God's." Jesus' interlocutors were not able to trap him, and they marveled at his reply.

Over the centuries, theologians and church leaders have referred to this episode when they talk about the relation of Christians to political and civic authority. For example, during the persecution in the 2nd century, Justin Martyr wrote that Christians worship God alone but should pay taxes and obey the civic authorities. Martin Luther, in the 16th century, distinguished between spiritual and earthly authorities. On the one hand, Christians should obey God, submit to God's authority and trust in God alone. On the other hand, they should obey earthly power and government, for they are ordained by God to protect civic order and to bring peace. For a long time, both the Catholic and Protestant traditions read this passage through the lens of a division of responsibilities between the church and civic authority. But such dualistic understanding has the danger of making Christians quiet and complacent, supporting the status quo.

With today's increasing concentration of wealth and widening gap between the rich and the poor, the ongoing debate on what is Caesar's and what is God's is highly relevant in our contemporary world. By addressing taxation, Jesus brings to the fore the notion of the yoke of colonial occupation and the question of economic justice. In the Roman tributary system, wealth and resources were channeled from the conquered peoples and provinces and funneled to the imperial metropolis. Today we have a global economic system that benefits the transnational capitalist elites while leaving many people out in the cold to struggle for themselves and their families. The Occupy movement uses the slogan "We are the 99%" to capture this gross economic inequity worldwide. In the U.S., the top 1% of income earners make 23% of all income, more than the bottom 50% in 2012, according to a study by economist Emmanuel Saez of the University of California, Berkeley. They use their wealth and power to lobby politicians and influence policies in order to keep their income tax and capital-gains tax low. With the ever widening gap between the haves and have-nots, many Christians are dissatisfied with keeping quiet and supporting the status quo.

Jesus did not tell his followers to acquiesce to Caesar's system but reminded them to give "to God what is God's." His Jewish audiences would have understood that everything comes from God, and therefore it is not right to worship both God and mammon.

The Hebrew prophets taught that those who have power should understand it as God's gift to them, given for the sake of God's people. Thus, it is in the tradition of the prophets that Jesus has denounced the powerful and the rich, and from which he can say in the Sermon on the Mount, "Blessed are the poor."

Christians live in the tension of the in-between or transitional space between the reign of Caesar and the reign of God. As such, we need to exercise our political agency to move our society closer to God's reign. So how can we imagine restorative justice for the many people who are wronged by the neoliberal economy? Some have suggested the formation of a world government and a retributive international taxation system. Others think that the buying of carbon credits by companies and individuals to offset the emission of carbon dioxide is a possible solution. While international taxation and carbon credits may not be enough to solve the world's gross injustice, they at least raise the prospect of measures that can be undertaken in this transitional space and time.

In John 18:36 Jesus says, "My kingdom is not of this world." He conceives of his power quite differently from that of earthly power. In his answer to the Pharisees, Jesus does not tell the people to challenge Roman rule directly, for he was not a revolutionary Zealot. Rather, he challenges the system by appealing to the people's religious and moral convictions and by raising their consciousness so that they might be able to distinguish between the spiritual and earthly authorities and decide what is Caesar's and what is God's.

Kwok Pui-lan *is the William F. Cole Professor of Christian Theology and Spirituality at the Episcopal Divinity School in Cambridge, Mass., and author of* Postcolonial Imagination and Feminist Theology.

ROGER LUNDIN

"Simon, are you asleep? Couldn't you keep watch for one hour?"

(MARK 14:37)

—•••—

This question draws us into the heart of a drama played out on a lonely night almost 2,000 years ago. Jesus posed it to Peter, one of his three disciples who had accompanied him to a corner in a garden called Gethsemane.

In Mark's Gospel we learn that a profound sorrow has gripped the soul of Jesus "even to death" and left him so "greatly distressed and troubled" that he asks Peter, James and John to wait while he slips off to pray "about a stone's throw" away (Luke 22:41).

There he falls to the ground and cries out, "Abba, Father. All things are possible. Remove this cup from me." These words of Jesus recall those of Isaiah: "Wake yourself, stand up, O Jerusalem, you who have drunk from the hand of the LORD the cup of his wrath … the cup of staggering" (Isaiah 51:17). It staggers Jesus to envision the wrath of God that is about to fall upon him through a series of events that will lead him to the Cross and leave him there to die. Still, despite his dread of the suffering to come, Jesus relents: "Yet not what I will, but what you will." He then rises, takes several strides and finds the three fast asleep. Wearily he asks Peter, "Couldn't you watch with me one hour?"

Three times Jesus prays in the garden that night, and each time his disciples abandon him to his sorrow as they sleep. In doing so, they set the pattern for Jesus' final hours, for from the garden to the Cross, no one—not even the one he calls "Abba, Father"—will appear to stand beside him in solidarity and sympathy.

Jesus is left to face his fate alone. He is spat upon and struck with mocking blows; he is reviled by crowds that shout, "Crucify him"; he is whipped and mocked by Roman soldiers; and as he is dying, passersby, priests deride him and the two men crucified beside him revile him. Not even God seems to watch with Jesus in his last hour: "And at the ninth hour Jesus cried with a loud voice, 'My God, my God, why have you forsaken me?'"

This final question from Golgotha returns us to the first one posed in Gethsemane, for both expose the dreadful anxiety that seized the soul of Jesus on his way to death. These questions also open our present day, in which many of us confront similar terrors in the darkness of the night, within the depths of the heart and even under the brightest of noonday suns.

Our modern questions often speak of a fear of being stranded as orphans in a godforsaken corner of one galaxy among the more than 100 billion other galaxies that glide through the skies above us. More than two centuries ago, the German writer Jean Paul captured this dread in a fable about a God-less world. In it Jesus appears at a church at midnight to speak to the dead who await him. "Christ, is there no God?" they ask in desperation, and he answers, "There is none." Having ascended to the suns and descended into the abyss, Christ has received no reply to his cry, "Father, where art Thou?" When he gazed into the divine eye, only an empty socket stared back. Dead infants stream into the darkened church and ask in desperation, "Jesus, have we no Father?" He can only report, "We are all orphans, you and I, we have no Father."

In the 19th century a number of people came to experience firsthand the spiritual fear Jean Paul imagined in the 18th century as the fantastic slowly became the commonplace, and men and women across Christendom began to feel the shock of having been orphaned through their loss of God.

Such experiences were chronicled in the fables and fiction of the day. "Our souls are like those orphans whose unwedded moth ers die in bearing them," lamented Herman Melville in *Moby-Dick* (1851). "The secret of our paternity lies in their grave, and we must there to learn it."

In Fyodor Dostoevsky's *The Brothers Karamazov* (1880), the death of God creates a world in which "all things are permitted" and nothing sacred remains, while in *The Gay Science* (1882), Friedrich Nietzsche's madman enters a village and wails, "God is dead. God remains dead. And we have killed him."

Across the Atlantic, in the same year, Emily Dickinson wrote a nine-line poem noting that those who died in the past ("Those— dying then") "Knew where they went—". It was to "God's Right Hand—" but "that hand is amputated now/ And God cannot be found—".

For countless millions, the past century—I am writing this in 2014, a hundred years after the start of the First World War— was one long, lonely journey from Gethsemane to Golgotha. Who was there to watch for even one hour with the men in the trenches of France? Who remained awake to stand alongside the boys, girls, women and men being packed into freight cars bound for Auschwitz? How many forsaken cries of dereliction have issued from homeless human hearts across the wired, wearying world in which we live?

We find one answer to such questions in a sermon preached by theologian Helmut Thielicke near midcentury in the ruins of war-ravaged Germany. To the question posed by the overwhelming anxiety felt by many in the modern world, Thielicke turns to the passion of Christ for a response, which he discovers in Jesus' final cry from the Cross.

He notes that when Jesus forsakenly calls out in despair, he speaks not as a homeless orphan but as a son who pleads with his father and brings his anxiety to him. If "I know Christ, I may rest assured that I am not alone with my anxiety; he has suffered it for me" and suffers it beside me. Two years before her death, Emily Dickinson told a neighbor that we "distrust" Jesus when he tells us about his Father and turn away when he shows us his home. "But when he confides to us that he is 'acquainted with Grief,' we listen," she said, "for that also is an Acquaintance of our own."

The one with whom not even his closest friends could "watch one hour" is the same one whose "acquaintance with Grief" keeps him ever alert to our anxieties, as we follow him on the path from Gethsemane to Golgotha—and beyond.

Roger Lundin *is the Arthur F. Holmes Professor of Faith and Learning at Wheaton College in Illinois, where he teaches American literature and modern European literature.*

VALERIE WEAVER-ZERCHER

"Am I leading a rebellion that you have come out with swords and clubs to capture me?"

(MARK 14:48)

----•••----

"Handcuff a nun" was likely not on the security officer's to-do list. But just before dawn one day in July 2012, the guard at a nuclear weapons facility in Tennessee came upon a baffling sight: three elderly folks hammering a concrete wall, spray-painting slogans about swords and plowshares and singing "This Little Light of Mine."

There was an element of the macabre and the absurd in their activities, what with the blood they had dripped on the ground and the crime-scene tape they had hung. And was it annoyance or fear that flickered in the guard's eyes when one of them began reading a passage of Scripture aloud and offered him a nub of bread?

The guard's supervisor arrived with body armor and an assault rifle. Calling in backup, they ordered Sister Megan Rice and her two friends to sit on the asphalt with their hands behind their backs. Soon the three pacifists would be wearing shackles and sentenced to several years behind bars. Two years later, a journalist would be denied a visit to Sister Megan in her New York prison because of "safety and security concerns."

Sister Megan is 85 years old. She has a heart condition.

Ever since I read an article about Sister Megan, she has slipped into my mind at random moments. Apparently, this is also the case for the creators of the Netflix series *Orange Is the New Black,* who based the character of Sister Ingalls, an upbeat nun incarcerated for civil disobedience at a nuclear facility, on Sister Megan. A good burglar she is, trespassing on federal property and imagination alike.

On that morning in July, Sister Megan and two fellow anti-nuclear activists had broken into Y-12, the holy of holies of American military might, which stores enough nuclear material to fuel more than 10,000 warheads. The uranium in every American warhead has been processed here. The uranium in the atomic bomb that killed more than 80,000 people in Hiroshima was processed here too. Here in this place, a nun, a housepainter and a Vietnam veteran hammered out a truth as embarrassing as it is terrifying: three senior citizens with wire cutters can break into a nuclear facility and putter around for two hours before anyone will notice.

An octogenarian pacifist nun humiliated a global superpower. No matter what you think of such activist theater, you cannot deny that fact. Is Sister Megan leading a rebellion, that men half her age grab their guns? Is she a bandit, that the U.S. government classifies her as a violent offender?

Yes.

No.

Like most good questions, these have more than one answer. Yes, the nun is leading a rebellion, but it's not the kind that a prison sentence can quash. Yes, she is a bandit, but the only items she pilfers are our senses of safety and respectability and national pride.

The incarcerated nun shuffles the same corridor of defenselessness and provocation as the Christ she serves. Like her Savior on the night before he was crucified, the nun is unarmed and dangerous. Like him, she has fashioned a vocation out of love of God and love of the Other, which imperil lesser loyalties to clan and state.

Seized in a garden after dark, Christ asked the armed crowd and his own dwindling band of followers a question that shames and illumines: "Am I leading a rebellion," said Jesus, "that you have come out with swords and clubs to capture me?" Just try answering such a rhetorical question without resorting to inanities. No, of course you're not leading a rebellion ... except, well, perhaps you are.

As soon as we open our mouths, we're exposed as frauds or cads. If we've been hanging around with Jesus the past few years, we could ace this test by reciting all those times he told us to love our enemies, pray for those who persecute us and turn the other cheek. "The answer is no!" we could hiss to Judas and his posse, or even to Peter, who has just hacked off some guy's ear. But we're too busy making ourselves scarce. Beating a hasty retreat, we confirm the opposite answer to Christ's question. Yes, a rebellion of sorts *is* going down, and we don't want to risk being charged as accomplices.

If, on the other hand, we are in the crew sent by the chief priests, we look just as ridiculous. Arresting this man allows us none of the bragging rights we've earned capturing other brigands, who at least had the good sense to carry a weapon and put up a fight. Turning himself in without so much as a curse, he is making our club-wielding selves feel a tad sheepish. So the answer is no, Jesus, you are obviously not an armed bandit; it's just that swords make us feel manly. Or is the answer yes, you've captured so many people's allegiance, and trespassed against so much sensible thought, that our bosses find you downright scary?

That Tennessee guard, the deserting disciples and Judas' cohorts all intuit the way the weak burgle the pretenses of the strong. They know in their bones that people who love as fiercely and profligately as Jesus and Sister Megan are dangerous indeed. Refusing to treat anyone as an enemy, they breach the logic of empires and revolutions.

Others, too, have committed these twin delinquencies of defenseless love and moral vision: 16th century Anabaptists, who called out the church's complicity with the state and went to their deaths as martyrs. Students of the White Rose in Nazi-era Germany, who strewed anti-Hitler pamphlets and were executed for treason. Unarmed civil rights demonstrators on the Edmund Pettus Bridge, whose heads were cracked open and limbs bloodied by police. The truck driver at my church, who was punched by a drunk man at a truck stop and promptly prayed with him and bought him breakfast.

The nun offered breakfast to the bewildered guard on that morning in July too. I imagine her pinching the bread between her arthritic fingers, plucking off a piece and proffering the body of Christ, broken, in the half-light of a Tennessee dawn.

Sister Megan packed a certain kind of heat when she trespassed that night, but it wasn't of the killing kind. On the night Jesus was arrested, he did too. Passed down the aisles of history, these are the weapons that Jesus carried, and they are still the elements that mark the uprising of the Christ: Bread. Scripture. Prayer. Blood freely given.

Valerie Weaver-Zercher *is a Mennonite essayist, the author of* Thrill of the Chaste *and the managing editor of trade books at Herald Press. Her work has appeared in the* Chicago Tribune *and the* Los Angeles Review of Books.

MITALI PERKINS

"Why were you searching for me? Didn't you know I had to be in my Father's house?"

(LUKE 2:49)

—•••—

A family journey. A missing child. Three days of separation and searching. A frantic mother scolding her 12-year-old son.

This story told by St. Luke features a plot and characters that are recognizable in most cultures and historical periods.

The only strange twist comes in the son's response to his mother.

It's easy to relate to Mary. The clan walks five days to reach Jerusalem in time for Passover. A day or so into the return trip, she discovers that Jesus isn't with Joseph and the other men. "He's not with the other children?" Joseph calls back.

They race back to the city, enlist relatives and scour venues where a Nazarene boy might lose track of time—marketplaces, playing fields, busy corners where tops and whistles are peddled.

Finally they find him. He's alive and well in the temple. Teaching, no less. Impressing a crowd with questions and answers.

As a mother, I would be torn between hugging and shaking the kid. He's 12, after all—on the verge of becoming a man. He should know better! But Mary's boy was lost. Not too long ago he was the baby she cradled. His voice cracks as he greets them, but his cheek is still smooth when she kisses it.

"Son, why have you treated us like this? Your father and I have been anxiously searching for you." Can you hear the relief and reprimand? Doesn't the reminder of a united parental front sound familiar?

The boy Jesus replies with two questions of his own. The first seems typical for a 12-year-old. But the other is different.

Islam's Quran describes a boy Jesus who created birds from clay and raised the dead to life. But the Gospel writers mostly skip his childhood altogether, which probably means they discovered the ordinary: crawling, walking, running, tripping, falling as a baby and toddler; acquiring language as most of us do, beginning to wield irony and metaphor as a teenager. Luke includes this one vignette, but it is brief, restrained, and it barely hints at the extraordinary. Jesus is not yet a full-fledged adolescent. He is 12, just embarking on the task of forming an identity.

"Why were you searching for me?"

The words ring with surprise. He is taken aback by his parents' lack of insight. They should have known! Why are they so worried? He realizes with a shock that he is old enough to see himself more clearly than the adults who have raised him.

His reaction is fairly universal. Age 12 is about when most of us dethrone our parents. We begin to know more about culture, more about trends, more even about ourselves than they do. The first question shows a Jesus coming of age much like every other tween in history. Seeing the limits of our parents' understanding propels us into maturity.

The incredulity of early adolescence lingers in Jesus' next question, but even as he asks it, he coins an odd phrase. "Didn't you know I had to be in my Father's house?"

None of his peers would use this name for the temple. A studious, devout 12-year-old may have put it like this: "Didn't you know I had to be in the temple?" A precocious boy might have retorted, "It's proper for a young man like me to be in the House of Adonai!"

In the Old Testament, God is called Father only a few times. But in the Gospels, "Father," or *Abba* in Aramaic, becomes Jesus' favorite way to address God. The phrase "my Father's house" is spoken three times in the Bible, and only by Jesus. He invents it here, as a boy. The second is in a scolding years later, as an adult: "To those who sold doves he said, 'Get these out of here! Stop turning my Father's house into a market!'" (John 2:16). And third, he uses it to encourage his friends. "My Father's house has many rooms; if that were not so, would I have told you that I am going there to prepare a place for you?" (John 14:2)

But the first time he talks about his Father's house, he is 12, and this is the place where people worship his Father. He belongs there; wherever his Father is revered is home.

The question rings with an understanding of his singular relationship with God. Jesus speaks it as the only begotten Son who shares genetic code with the Divine Daddy. He is the biological child; the rest of us are adopted.

To write the one story featuring Jesus as a young protagonist, Luke must have interviewed Mary. "What was he like as a boy? Did he do any miracles?"

She recalled that long-ago family trip to Jerusalem. The miracle she described was a young Jesus beginning to grasp the mystery of his intertwined identity. His first question revealed his humanity: "Why were you searching for me?" But the second showed that Jesus was divine and unlike any other child on the planet: "Didn't you know I had to be in my Father's house?"

No, Jesus, we did not. But now we do.

Mitali Perkins *writes novels for young readers. She is the author of nine books, including* Tiger Boy *and* Bamboo People.

EUGENE CHO

"Can the blind lead the blind?"

(LUKE 6:39)

The question appears ridiculous. I mean, seriously: How can the blind lead the blind? Our quick cerebral answer is an emphatic no.

But like everything that Jesus says, this demands a closer examination and an even closer introspection.

To understand the context, we need to understand the adversaries of Jesus. In other words, Jesus wasn't liked by everybody. Nope. In fact, I think it's fair to say that not only was he misunderstood but he was vilified and even demonized by the religious leaders of the times. Yes, I said "demonized." While there were various religious groups, the two main groups were the Pharisees and the Sadducees. And yes, they were both incredibly religious and had both similarities and differences—which made them rivals. The Pharisees are often categorized as particularly religious, middle-class business-minded men who were better connected or accessible to the larger community. The Sadducees, on the other hand, were mostly wealthy and politically inclined and thus worked hard to hold prominent political positions and the majority of the

Sanhedrin—the ruling council of Israel that comprised 70 men and one high priest. Both of these groups vehemently opposed Jesus. In fact, one of the rare occasions the Pharisees and the Sadducees worked together was during the trial of Jesus that ultimately led to the Crucifixion of Jesus.

Now, mind you, these were religious and civic leaders. Leaders who were supposed to be in tune with God's word and thus God's character. They were leaders who were supposed to guide, love, protect and shepherd people. Instead, they exemplified the abuse of spiritual power. Did they not read the Torah and clearly read God's heart for the poor, the widows and orphans? God's invitation for integrity, holiness and humility? God's demand for fairness and justice? Instead, they grew blind in their abusive power and hunger for privilege and wealth.

Can the blind lead the blind?

Absolutely. Jesus is not saying they cannot. In fact, this is the tragic point that he is trying to illuminate. An urgent wake-up call—to both religious leaders and followers, then and now. These religious leaders were feared, revered and elevated, which only exacerbates the dangerous cycle as leaders are blinded by this reverence and their followers likewise duped. And Jesus does not hold back on his criticism of the religious leaders. In several instances, Jesus calls them "broods of vipers" (Matthew 3:7, 12:34, 23:33) to convey their poisonous, toxic and venomous nature and calls out their "blindness" (John 9).

Jesus answers his own question with a question, saying, "Shall they not both fall into the ditch?" For many readers, it's possible we don't quite understand the significance or the real danger of ditches. A ditch from our perspective may be a little bump in the road. Nothing harmful at all. That's not at all what Jesus meant when he gave this metaphor. A more accurate translation for ditch may actually be "pit." Imagine deep and dangerous and that's more like what Jesus meant. People could fall into these pits, hurt themselves, or worse, be unable to come out and thus experience death. Rare but true.

It actually makes sense that the Pharisees and Sadducees vilified Jesus. He was a threat to their worldview, their way of life, their power structures and their privilege. Jesus was the complete antithesis of these religious leaders. He wasn't seduced by this power and privilege. If anything, Jesus practiced a lifestyle and commitment of servanthood and what I call downward mobility that contradicts the allure of upward mobility that was so pervasive in the power-hungry endeavors of the Pharisees and Sadducees—and if we're honest, that's also pervasive in our culture today, defining significance and status through wealth, materialism, fame and power.

The incarnation is the story of how Jesus humbled himself and chose not to exercise his divine rights, instead choosing to take on flesh and bone and assume full humanity—being fully God but also fully man.

Born in a manger to simple commoners, Jesus assumed a simple lifestyle as a carpenter. Throughout his life, he owned nothing but the things he could take with him. His life is the mind-boggling, heart-compelling, countercultural story of downward mobility.

This is a lesson and a story we all have to get behind. This is the Jesus we have to get behind—the Jesus of downward mobility. He is not the Jesus of bling-bling, the Jesus of total-prosperity theology, a Jesus of exclusivity and elitism, a Jesus of health and wealth, or the Jesus of "send $49 and we'll mail you this special anointed cloth for your personal miracle."

Jesus was best exemplified by his self-proclamation in John 10:11, 14: "I am the good shepherd." Jesus was both tender and gentle and yet also fierce in his pursuit of justice. Jesus didn't just speak of these things; he demonstrated these things in how he lived, how he loved and how he welcomed the stranger, the marginalized, the leper, the widow, the prostitute and the sick. Jesus reflected justice in how he approached the powers and systems of his age, how he confronted religious leaders, how he embraced, welcomed and empowered women and how he confronted ethnic biases and prejudices.

Can the blind lead the blind?

The answer is yes, and this is why we must keep asking the important questions of "Who are we following?" and "Where are they leading us?" and perhaps for those in power and authority, "Where are we leading people to?"

May we lead people to Jesus himself who proclaims, "I am the way, the truth, and the life." May we lead people to follow in his steps.

Eugene Cho *is the senior pastor of Quest Church in Seattle, founder of One Day's Wages—a grassroots movement of people, stories and actions to alleviate extreme global poverty—and author of* Are We More in Love With the Idea of Changing the World Than Actually Changing the World?

LECRAE

"Why do you call me, 'Lord, Lord,' and do not do what I say?"

(LUKE 6:46)

This is a serious question for Jesus.

"Not everyone who says to me, 'Lord, Lord,' will enter the kingdom of heaven," Jesus said in Matthew's Gospel, "but only the one who does the will of my Father who is in heaven. Many will say to me on that day, 'Lord, Lord, did we not prophesy in your name and in your name drive out demons and in your name perform many miracles?' Then I will tell them plainly, 'I never knew you. Away from me, you evildoers!'"

In Scripture, when something is repeated, especially a name, it shows an emotional connection, a deeper sense of meaning. When David mourned over his son's death, he cried, "Absalom, Absalom." There was a sense of passion behind that.

As followers of Jesus, it is easy to feel that emotional connection to God and yet still not do what he says. This is a good diagnostic question for any Christian to ask—at the end of the day, does my life reflect that I have embraced Jesus as the Lord of it?

It is easy to want to hold on to our own lives. We want purpose, a sense of doing the right thing. "I'm cool with some of the Gospel stuff," we say, "but just not in certain areas of my life."

I heard this question clearly when I graduated from college. My graduation was an amazing moment for my family, my community. In my early childhood we lived on a subsidized income, with government assistance—at one point when I was growing up, my mother was making $14,000 a year. Now I had made it out of the hood, so to speak.

But when I graduated, I felt a pull inside me, calling my attention to the fact that people in the urban community, people in the hood, needed a vision for what they too could become. I knew that I could be an example. I faced a question: Do I move back?

I remember a friend challenged me with Jesus' words: "Why do you call me, 'Lord, Lord,' and do not do what I say?" All signs pointed to my moving into this urban community. I knew that it was frowned upon. "Man, you moved on!" I could hear people say. But I felt like I had to lay my volition down. I really felt burdened to do this, that it was really something that God would have me do.

And so I moved into Binghamton, one of the toughest areas of Memphis. And it wasn't a "Yay, this is awesome" moment. It was a difficult time. There were multiple murders that I had to wrestle with, and all kinds of different issues that I had to put up with. But the fruit of it is still being produced.

Kids who were 11 at the time had the odds stacked against them. Now they are 18 years old and they are enrolled in school, and they are upstanding members of their community. When I first moved there, I met kids who had never seen a wedding before. For them to see my wedding pictures … they had never seen anything like it.

It painted new pictures for them, new paradigms and a new value system. It helped them say, "Wait—I didn't know we could go to college. I didn't know I could think about any of these things, but seeing your life has made this a reality."

Following Jesus wasn't just about me. It was about them. Laying my will down for Jesus was laying my life down for others.

I can go to Ferguson, Mo., to advocate for justice, I can give money to the Red Cross after the Haiti earthquake, and I can write Christian music, but have I ultimately given up my will? I always have to ask myself, Do I really lay down every aspect of my life?

And even when you are doing all the right things, there's still something more. It is possible to call God "Lord," to feel emotionally connected to faith, to do the altruistic things and still not want God.

That is what Jesus is getting at. Are you laying down your will? Or are you using Jesus to get what you want?

It comes down to something big: Do you really want God?

Lecrae is a Grammy Award—winning hip-hop artist. In 2014 he became the first artist in Billboard *chart history to occupy the top album spot on both the* Gospel Albums *and* Billboard Top 200 *lists.*

OTIS MOSS III

"Do you see this woman?"

(LUKE 7:44)

—•••—

Questions Jesus poses often haunt our spirit and linger beyond the time of comfortable reflection. Like splinters lodged in the flesh, the sacred question or questions refuse to release us until we gather enough courage to hear what God proposes.

What is strange and disconcerting about Jesus is the fact that he rarely makes demands. The style of teaching he engages in is not rote memorization or indoctrination but Socratic, propositional and inductive. The listener is invited to explore and come to a conclusion. It is the desire of Christ for his audience to reach a conclusion and not be told what to think.

Stories, sayings, reversals, parables and other forms of teaching used by Jesus are not good teaching tools for people who seek simplistic answers. Jesus teaches but requires more of the listener. We are invited to join the journey, wrestle with our assumptions, confront our spiritual bigotry and struggle with the humbling mystery and profound profundity of God.

This is hard faith, especially for the modern reader. We want the speaker to tell us what to think. We want our stories neat and tidy, without complication, and we do not want questions designed to coerce us beyond easy answers.

This is the life and ministry of Jesus. He is a walking mobile university, a theological gadfly, a spiritual teacher and Savior who cannot be contained by tradition, conformity or assimilation. Jesus is loose in the world quietly upending all assumptions, ideas and concepts we hold true.

On the surface, to the casual reader, this simple question, "Do you see this woman?," is nothing more than an action statement designed to get Simon, one of Jesus' disciples, to turn his head and look at the woman, who, with tears and determination, wipes the feet of Jesus. It would be a tragedy to skip over this question as a rhetorical flourish and miss this world-altering proposition from this country preacher from the plain of Palestine named Jesus.

"Do you see this woman?" Do you see this person who has been dismissed by Rome and your theological doctrine as a nonentity? Do you see this woman, nameless to all the men, defined as sinner, rebellious, unclean and of low moral wattage because men who idolize their gender have scandalized her humanity? Do you see this woman? I want you to see this woman beyond your constructs, beliefs, cultural dogma and foolish ideology. I want you to see this woman. Look, Simon, she is impoverished, oppressed and wounded, yet she has given great service to God.

Jesus forces us to look where we do not want to look. Our necks are held in place and our eyes are opened to the suffering and humanity of one of our own. We see this woman, not as an outsider, but as us. We see this woman and are brought to tears because we are complicit in her condition.

Do you see this woman? Do you see her standing on corners in cities holding a sign soliciting kindness? Do you see her crossing the southern border with children in tow, running from danger and hoping for a new future? Do you see this woman, not yet an adult, walking streets late at night flagging down cars looking for men who cruise the city to support the oldest profession? Do you see her making choices between food or rent, education or employment, health or safety, love or security? Do you see her never able to make ends meet but always smiling with joy for her children?

The question is not just Do you see her? but Do we know we are her? "Do you see this woman?"

Otis Moss III *is the senior pastor of Trinity United Church of Christ in Chicago.*

DHYANCHAND CARR

"Which of these three, do you think, proved neighbor to the man who fell among the robbers?"

(LUKE 10:36, RSV)

In Jesus' day, Jewish travelers going between Judaea and Galilee normally avoided passing through Samaria. The Samaritans were a mixed race as a result of the Assyrian invasion and occupation of aliens in their land, and they were also following a syncretistic religion, some of which had fertility-cult leanings. However, they also claimed their Israelite heritage and faithfulness to the Law of Moses, and they believed that the Messiah would come to redeem the world.

Jesus, however, traveled up and down through Samaria. During one such journey, he met and talked with kindness to the Samaritan woman and through her witness won over her entire village. Another time a village refused him overnight lodging, but this did not cloud his mind with prejudice toward the Samaritans, nor did he endorse the general Jewish dislike of Samaritans. Jesus was also troubled about the vast regime of purity and pollution laws that Jewish people lived by. These laws were a barrier for interpersonal expressions of concern, across interethnic and interfaith boundaries.

In this parable—Jesus' response to the question "Who is my neighbor?," posed by a lawyer—it is the Samaritan who shows compassion toward the injured traveler, not the religious leaders. The story highlights the inhibitions of the priest and the Levite who crossed over to the other side of the street and continued down the road to Jericho after finishing their responsibilities at the temple. Purity and pollution laws forbade participation in temple rituals for an entire week if a person had touched a dead body. The priest and Levite likely feared the death of the stricken traveler and avoided helping him.

In this context, clearly the parable of the Good Samaritan went beyond teaching sympathy and care for an injured stranger. The story told of the Samaritan who extended assistance to a Jewish person—remarkable because Jewish people looked down on Samaritans and usually avoided any kind of dealing with the Samaritans. The priest and the Levite shared ethnicity with the injured traveler, but in all probability their preoccupation with the purity laws of their scriptures got in the way of their responding with human kindness. For Jesus, being a neighbor means to take on the mandated obligation of the next of kin, and it is an ethnically estranged person who performs that duty to the wounded traveler.

What message does this have for us Christians today? In India, Christians are a small minority—we form around 2% of the total population. It is common for us to differentiate our identity by adopting names and practices different from those of our majority neighbors, the Hindus. But we do not stop here. Out of proportion to our numbers we enjoy the clout of a vast number of educational institutions founded by the missionaries. These institutions are sustained by government grants, i.e., by taxpayers' money. But as management rights are with the church, we exclude those of other faiths. Are we being "good neighbors" in such circumstances?

It is a fact that many of our Christian service institutions are increasingly staffed almost exclusively by those of our faith. As a teacher involved for many years in training ministers who would one day manage Christian mission service institutions, I repeatedly asked if they would treat non-Christian job applicants on par with Christian applicants. The answer was always no. Some said they would lose their jobs if they did not "safeguard" the institutions for "Christians only." Others argued that it could not be wrong to favor Christian applicants; after all, these are "our institutions" in a country of a majority of Hindus. They forget that they are sustained by the taxes of this majority community.

Jesus wanted the lawyer to understand that being a neighbor would mean going beyond the restrictions of formal religion. When he recognized that the Samaritan was the real neighbor, Jesus told him, "Go and do thou likewise." This seems to have a message for those of us Protestant Christians who insist that salvation is by faith alone.

Reflecting on the wider implications, the Apostle Paul in Ephesians says that Christ died to make peace between the Jews and the Gentiles, by breaking down the dividing wall of separation. This challenges all of us to think afresh about our Christian duty to break down walls that continue to exist. Christ paved the way for the New Humanity.

All of us have sinned and fallen short of the glory of God.

However, God overcomes this hurdle and reaches out to us. Our religion is utilitarian. There is little desire to serve God. In spite of this, the book of Romans says, Christ died for us when we were yet sinners and even enemies of God.

So maybe, rather than simply drawing a lesson to be compassionate toward the less fortunate, we should reflect on the great and immeasurable love of God which transcends all legitimate and difficult barriers and reaches out to us. The only way to break down these walls and barriers erected by culture, endorsed by religion and enforced by ethnic and racial divisions is to keep alive the dream of a New Human Community.

Dhyanchand Carr *is a liberation theologian in Tamil Nadu, India. He is the author of* Sword of the Spirit *and* Reading the Bible With New Eyes.

GRACE JI-SUN KIM

"Which of you fathers, if your son asks for a fish, will give him a snake instead?"

(LUKE 11:11)

—•••—

Praying is difficult.

I will never forget receiving a frantic call from my sister from Canada, a call I never imagined I would receive in my lifetime. My sister said our mom had gone to the doctor with some health issues and they had found that she had Stage IV lung cancer.

Cancer is more dreaded the younger the patient.

My mother was only 63 and healthy. It was always my dad who had health issues. My mom was the healthiest one in our family. She took care of my dad, my sister and me when we were ill. She always ate a healthy diet, exercised and never smoked. My mom even ate all the cancer-fighting foods like raw broccoli, soybeans, green tea, garlic and leafy vegetables.

Despite all that, she developed Stage IV lung cancer. And the doctors said that at Stage IV, there isn't much left to do to help cancer patients. Our family plummeted into the depths of despair and sorrow.

As Christians, our family prayed for healing. But during months of prayer, her health grew worse. She had a stroke that left her mute and largely immobile.

We prayed and we felt that God did not hear our prayers. In similar situations, many Christians have prayed fervently and watched as loved ones died. And yet Christians continue to pray. Why do we pray when it appears that God is not answering?

Prayer may be viewed as a free store where we grab for anything we want. Many of us see God as a divine version of Santa Claus who grants our wishes. However, we soon recognize that we do not see our prayers answered by God in the ways we ask. During those times, we feel anxious and unsettled as we try to understand why God does not grant our wishes. There is only silence and then more silence. Our family, friends and church members prayed for my mother. And God did not answer our prayers.

In the midst of this self-doubt, I come to this passage in Luke and I make it my own.

Jesus assures us that as a parent would give children what they request, God will do likewise. Parents always want the best for their children: the best schools, the best food, the best of the best. That is how Jesus is comparing his relationship to us in this passage, that our relationship with God resembles the parent-child relationship. Just as a parent loves a child, how much more does God love us?

We persist in prayer because Jesus is saying that if a human parent would not give a scorpion for an egg to a beloved child, then neither will God. Why? Because God is the "ultimate good," the one who is greater than all human parents. Jesus continues, "If you then, who are evil, know how to give good gifts to your children, how much more will the heavenly Father give the Holy Spirit to those who ask him!" This is the "how much more"—if evil humans can give "good gifts"—won't the great and good God do even more?

Out of my pain at the illness and death of my mother and my feeling that our prayers went unanswered, I find this question comforting. Jesus asks other questions intended to make his audience, to make us, uncomfortable. Jesus calls us to examine our lives and search our inner souls to respond to his questions. However, this question about eggs and scorpions encourages us to hang on. It makes us realize that God's love is greater than anything that we can imagine. In our own impatient way, we need to rely on God and wait upon God's time.

Prayer is a matter of faith. We believe and trust that God's goodness will be granted to us in prayer, even when the immediate answers are "No" or "Not yet." This is part of the human agony of prayer. The waiting (as we know all too well!) is the hardest part.

We recognize that God is not a cosmic, divine Amazon.com. God does not answer all prayers the way we want. As he faced his death, Jesus prayed in the Garden, "this cup be removed." God did not. However, Jesus continued to follow faithfully God's will.

Prayer involves trust. When Jesus tells us to ask, knock and see, he is speaking more about our trusting God than about our receiving things from God. We need to trust God and try to discern God's will. Trust God in times of pain. Trust God in times of death. As our trust in God deepens, our prayers begin to change. We become the children who will pray the prayer that gives us some peace and understanding. Prayer leads us to the mystery of God and we cannot fully understand God's being, will, actions and mercy toward us.

We all face death: our own death and the death of loved ones. As I look back upon the death of my mother, I wonder if rather than praying for death to wait or visit my mother in a decade, perhaps I should have prayed as my seminary classmate did when she was diagnosed with cancer. She prayed to God, "Yes, why not me?" She accepted her cancer with grace and trust in God. In so doing, she found peace. There is mystery in prayer.

At the end of our journey of life, we fall before the face of God in awe of the mystery in the fullness of God's compassion, mercy and grace. God's heart is bountiful and deep. And we begin to recognize this in our prayers.

This passage in Luke reminds us that we are not to give up on prayer but that we are to pray without ceasing. We need to come before God's mercy and pray in all the circumstances we face. In prayer, what we are truly seeking, whether we know it or not, is God. For it is through prayer that we recognize God's grace toward us which sustains us even as we walk through the shadowed valley of death. The need to pray comes from the knowledge that God asks us to pray in order that we might know and trust and live with and for God.

Prayer is difficult. It is a discipline brought forth from faith, hope and trust. Jesus Christ shows us God's love. This is grace, freely given to us. This is the good news.

Grace Ji-Sun Kim *is an associate professor of theology at Earlham School of Religion and the author of* Colonialism, Han, and the Transformative Spirit *and* Embracing the Other. *She is a minister in the Presbyterian Church (USA).*

CARDINAL TIMOTHY DOLAN

"Do you think that these Galileans were worse sinners than all the other Galileans because they suffered this way?"

(LUKE 13:2)

---•••---

Remember the best seller *When Bad Things Happen to Good People*, by Rabbi Harold Kushner? Even though the book was published more than 30 years ago, it's still popular today, as Rabbi Kushner explores one of the central mysteries that has perplexed men and women for millennia. Why do the just suffer? Why does tragedy strike? How can we explain why a loving God would cause such pain to those who love him?

Jesus asked the same question:

Do you think that these Galileans were worse sinners than all the other Galileans because they suffered this way?

It has been 2,000 years since Jesus posed this question to his closest friends and followers, and we're still grappling with its implications today. We seem to jump to the conclusion that if someone has a setback, sickness or struggle, that person must deserve it, because they asked for it! They're sinners, and a just God is punishing them.

So when I visit a friend in the hospital facing major surgery for a life-threatening condition, she wonders out loud, "Why is this happening to me? What have I done to deserve this?" I hear the same question when I visit a funeral home to comfort a wife who has just lost her loving husband, a police officer killed in the line of duty, leaving her with three small children to raise on her own. When my own niece, not yet a teenager, was fighting cancer and undergoing intense chemotherapy with no guarantee that she would live, I found myself looking to heaven and saying, "Why, God? How can you allow this? What can this poor little girl have done to justify this pain that she is enduring?"

That same faulty way of thinking—that those who suffer somehow deserve their fate because of their sins—often creeps uninvited into how we perceive those less economically or socially fortunate than ourselves, doesn't it? When we pass a panhandler huddled in a doorway, or see migrant workers standing on a street corner hoping for a day's work, or hear of a devastating fire that kills a family living in a run-down house without smoke detectors, we might be tempted to think that they must have been doing something wrong, illegal or immoral to deserve their fate.

It is natural to want an explanation for life's mysteries, to seek out the why for things that are unknown and unknowable. Perhaps in some ways it gives us comfort to think that people deserve their fate, as we fool ourselves into believing that we, because we are good people living faultless lives, will somehow immunize ourselves against ill fortune and keep ourselves and those we love free from such sorrow and heartache.

But with this haunting and provocative question in Luke's Gospel, Jesus rebuts the faulty logic that leads to the conclusion that suffering and tragedy come only because we are sinners.

Remember the setting. This is the explanation his followers gave to the reports that the tyrannical Pontius Pilate had butchered people in Jerusalem. They must have done something wrong to upset God and deserve such a bloody end, people thought. This misguided way of thinking was as common in the days of Jesus as it seems to be today.

Jesus corrects them—and us. What he explains is that God, his loving and merciful Father, who he told us was *Our Father* as well, does not act like that. He is not a mean and vindictive God. While Jesus does not give us a full explanation of *why* the innocent have to suffer, he sure tells us why they did *not*. They did *not* suffer because God was mad at them for their sins.

The best answer Jesus gives to the nagging question of suffering would come from his own example, on a hill called Calvary, on a Friday strangely termed "Good," when Pilate would again spill blood—the precious blood of Jesus himself.

Come to think of it, his Father and ours would definitively answer the question three days later, the first Easter, when he raises Jesus from the dead!

Cardinal Timothy Dolan *is the Roman Catholic Archbishop of New York.*

STEPHANIE PAULSELL

"What is the kingdom of God like? What shall I compare it to?"

(LUKE 13:18)

—•••—

Jesus asks an especially expansive question in Luke 13:18: "What is the kingdom of God like? What shall I compare it to?" Jesus answers his own question with a parable: the Kingdom of God is like a tiny mustard seed that grows into a tree so large that birds make nests in its branches. He then asks the question again: "To what shall I compare the kingdom of God?" This time the Kingdom of God is like the yeast that a woman mixes into her flour to leaven it.

Jesus asks the same question twice and answers with a different parable each time, suggesting that his answers are not the only ones this question might evoke. By offering multiple answers, he invites us to imagine our own parables. What else do we see around us that might evoke the hiddenness of God's Kingdom in our midst, its secret growth? What else can we think of that starts out small and then grows and expands until it is large enough to be lived in or nourishing enough to sustain our lives?

Maybe the Kingdom of God is like a young Muslim girl in Pakistan who grows up to devote herself to the education of girls. Maybe the Kingdom of God is like the book that first awakened her love of learning. Maybe the Kingdom of God is like the idea that led the author of that book to toss a lifeline of words out into the future for that young girl to catch.

When religion is discussed and debated in our culture, it is often portrayed as a set of beliefs that we either do or do not accept, beliefs that demand certain choices about politics or science or sex. Rarely is religion portrayed as imaginative, creative work. Jesus' question reminds us that living a life of faith requires imagination. Jesus does not ask: What *is* the Kingdom of God? He asks: What is the Kingdom of God *like?* He invites us to cultivate, as the theologian David Tracy once put it, an analogical imagination. He invites us to think with things we can see and touch about things we can only imagine.

As many commentators have noted, Jesus' question about what the Kingdom of God is like follows a story about outraged opposition to Jesus and his ministry. Luke places Jesus' parables where they can offer encouragement where it is most needed. Even when it seems otherwise, these parables suggest, the Kingdom of God is doing its secret work in hidden places. The ordinary miracles of growth and transformation are still happening even when we cannot yet see the outcome.

Hidden within Jesus' invitation to imagine what God's Kingdom is like is a call not only to create but to experiment with our own parables. Dorothy Day, founder of the Catholic Worker movement, imagined the Kingdom of God to be like a home where anyone could find a meal, a place to rest and the company of others. The works of mercy are practiced in her houses of hospitality to this day. Martin Luther King Jr. imagined the Kingdom of God to be like a society where all children thrive, all children are free, and all children are cherished and protected. His radical capacity to imagine the Kingdom of God hidden, like yeast, even in the midst of a violent, unjust society still challenges our nation to change.

Believing is often lifted up as the quintessential religious stance. But imagining is just as important—indeed, believing depends upon our ability to imagine a God we cannot see or to feel the claim on us of the strange, ancient words of Scripture.

And imagination is at the heart of the ethical choices to which Jesus calls us. During the last brutal months of World War I, the novelist Virginia Woolf wrote in her diary that the willingness to kill must be a failure of the imagination—an inability to imagine another person's life and what it might become. The imaginative work at the heart of the life of faith challenges us to cultivate our capacity to imagine lives other than our own—and to care about them enough to take them into account as we make choices about how we will live.

What is the Kingdom of God like? To what shall we compare it? With this open, inviting question, Jesus opens a space for more and more answers. The Kingdom of God is like a drop of indigo in white paint, a pinch of saffron in a pot of rice. It is like a healing dose of medicine in a suffering body, a fragment of hope in the midst of fear. The Kingdom of God is pervasive and transformative, and once it has been added, it cannot be separated out.

As Jesus knew, being able to imagine God's Kingdom in the ordinary things of our lives awakens our attention to the signs of it, everywhere. Looking for the Kingdom of God hidden in our midst, we may find it, and finding it, we may be changed by it, and changed, we may become like the yeast in the bread, the seed in the ground. Through his question, Jesus invites us into the creative work of the life of faith which renders hidden things visible and brings new ways of living into the world.

Stephanie Paulsell *is the Susan Shallcross Swartz Professor of the Practice of Christian Studies at Harvard Divinity School.*

"Or suppose a woman has ten silver coins and loses one. Doesn't she light a lamp, sweep the house and search carefully until she finds it?"

(LUKE 15:8)

—•••—

"There are two ways of thinking and of having faith: we can fear to lose the saved, and we can want to save the lost," Pope Francis observed in his homily on Feb. 15, 2015, at St. Peter's Basilica in Rome.

The Pope clearly had in mind the struggle the Church is facing in these days between a legalistic approach and the more pastoral path he is advocating. "Even today it can happen that we stand at the crossroads of these two ways of thinking," he continued as he referred to the current debate in the Church. "For Jesus, what matters above all is reaching out to save those far off, healing the wounds of the sick, restoring everyone to God's family. And this is scandalous to some people!" But, the Pope continued, "Jesus is not afraid of this kind of scandal. He does not think of the closed-minded who are scandalized even by a work of healing, scandalized before any kind of openness, by any action outside of their mental and spiritual boxes, by any caress or sign of tenderness which does not fit into their usual thinking and their ritual purity."

The Parable of the Lost Coin (Luke 15:8–10) is another account of the resistance Jesus faced from those easily scandalized by his unconventional outreach to save the lost. Unique to the Evangelist Luke, this parable is the second of three parables (Lost Sheep, Lost Coin, Lost Son) told in response to Jesus' critics who complain, "This man welcomes sinners and eats with them." It also offers important insights about what is at stake in saving the lost, from God's point of view. The emphasis from the outset is on God's joy in finding the lost. It is a fresh invitation to those easily scandalized by God's mercy to deepen their faith and to develop their way of thinking about what motivates God and how God acts in human events.

Luke gives a rich color and texture to that joy by relating it to the euphoria that overcomes the woman who has found the coin she lost. We are told she "lights a lamp, sweeps the house and searches carefully until she finds the coin." One gets the impression that she is fixated on finding the coin and ready to turn the house upside down to recover it, not caring about the mess her search creates. She can deal with that later.

Scholars have speculated on the significance of losing this coin. We are told it is one of 10 coins. This could mean it represents 10 days of pay and therefore the family's entire savings.

I prefer the more imaginative interpretation that identifies the 10 coins as part of her headdress. Even today, there is a custom of women in the Middle East wearing coins on their headdresses, particularly single women, with the coins representing their families' wealth and therefore the dowry they would bring to the marriage. As someone humorously remarked, "The coins on the headdress are like money in the bank. They are there to create a little interest!"

So the coins represent her future. In finding the lost one, she rejoices as one whose future was in doubt but is now restored. Her exhilaration stands in contrast to the desperation that gripped her heart at losing the coin.

Jesus is telling the leaders that this is God's joy. The return of the sinner is not just about the sinner's future but God's. Saving the sinner is important to God's plan, God's future. The Father rejoices not only because what was lost is now found but also because what was found has an impact on how God's Kingdom will unfold.

With this parable, Jesus extends an extraordinary invitation to the Pharisees and the scribes. He summons them to deal with sinners in an entirely new and creative way. This means far more than "going easy" on sinners or offering them cheap mercy or forgiveness or being content with knowing the law and enforcing it. No, Jesus calls them to become excited about what God is doing to redeem what was lost, and to join in building the future of God's Kingdom. In Jesus' vision, saving the lost is not just about saving the lost. It is about refitting them into God's future plans, which were thwarted by Adam's sin. If this means fixating only on the lost—turning the house upside down and creating a mess for a while—then so be it. These consequences are secondary to searching out and recovering the lost. The present mess gives way to redeeming and restoring the future as God envisions it.

In moral matters today, some see a high-stakes debate between proponents of an easy mercy and the partisans of the rigorous enforcement of the law. In his parables, Jesus moves well beyond such a debate. His words are not designed to win an argument but to change hearts. In revealing the Father's heart, Jesus invites his critics to appreciate that the sinner's salvation is also the salvation of God's promised future.

He also urges them to see that God's future includes them as well. Jesus cares about their salvation too. These critics too are part of God's future. They are like the elder son in the next parable. The father goes out and invites him into the house for the celebration. The joy of the father is not complete if this son is absent. They are also like the 99 sheep left behind as the shepherd searches for the one that is lost.

A priest of Chicago recently shared with me that he once asked a shepherd if it was realistic for a shepherd to leave the 99 in search of the lost one. " Yes," he was told, "and when he returns the one to the fold, the other sheep realize that he will do the same for each of them, and as a result, they more tightly bond with the shepherd as one they trust."

In the end, Jesus presses his critics to view the sinner's return from God's point of view but also with a good dose of humility, inviting them to a deeper relationship of trust in God, who is always ready to make the same effort on their behalf when they are lost.

And, in drawing closer to God in deeper trust, they too will be saved.

Archbishop Blase Cupich *is the Roman Catholic Archbishop of Chicago and the Chancellor of the Catholic Extension Society.*

NAIM ATEEK

"Were not all ten cleansed? Where are the other nine? Has no one returned to give praise to God except the foreigner?"

(LUKE 17:17-18)

The Gospels contain many stories in which Jesus Christ offered healing and wholeness to sick people, including lepers. But only the Gospel of Luke relates the story of the 10 lepers.

Jesus was on his way to Jerusalem, and as he was about to enter a village, he met 10 lepers. They shouted from a distance, "Jesus, have mercy on us." Jesus told them to go and show themselves to the priests as the law prescribed. As they went on their way, they were healed. Nine of them were Jews, and one was a Samaritan. The Samaritan immediately returned to Jesus and was praising God in a loud voice; he prostrated himself before Jesus and expressed his thanks. Then Jesus asked, "Were not ten made clean? But the other nine, where are they? Was none of them found to return and give praise to God except this foreigner?" Then Jesus addressed the Samaritan, "Get up and go on your way; your faith has made you well."

Enmity between Samaritans and Jews was pronounced during Jesus' time. They did not relate to one another. They lived in separate sections of the country. They negated each other socially and religiously. Each held the other in contempt. The story of the 10 lepers also does not tell us who witnessed this episode—we assume that at least Jesus' disciples were there.

Jesus posed three consecutive questions to stimulate the thinking of those around: "Were not all ten cleansed? Where are the other nine? Has no one returned to give praise to God except the foreigner?"

Oftentimes, although we know the answer, we ask questions for the benefit of listeners in order to help them evaluate, correct or confirm their positions and beliefs. Questions can also help us ponder the reality around us and assist us in facing the challenges that arise. Questions can also take us beyond what our eyes can see and allow us to confront and contemplate the deeper meanings. For beyond the physical sight lie deeper insights that questions can help us comprehend. When Jesus raised the questions, was he evoking a more profound reflection? In other words, was he asking, "Where is the 'arrogant majority'?" "How come only the 'vulnerable minority' appreciate the blessing?"

Jesus' third question carries within it the crux of the issue. On one level, there is the sad fact that after they were cured, nine lepers failed to return and thank Jesus. Jesus was, therefore, expressing an endemic problem that reflects a common spiritual dearth found in many humans, namely, when we attain what we want and desire, we neglect to recognize the source of our blessing.

On a deeper level, however, the crucial question is to expose the prevalent and ubiquitous racism between Jews and Samaritans. Jesus used the word *foreigner,* which was commonly employed to refer to an outsider. By merely posing the question Jesus managed to turn the stereotyping of foreigners on its head. The so-called despised and disgusting Samaritan was the only one to return and thank Jesus. The Samaritan who was supposed to be a heretic, immoral and spiritually void, turned out to be the most acutely religious and spiritual. He modeled true faith and morality.

More poignantly, when Jesus told the Samaritan "Get up (stand up) and go on your way, your faith has made you well," Jesus lifted him up in more than one sense. He lifted up his spirit, acknowledged his self-worth and showed respect to his religious faith. Jesus embraced the Samaritan on an equal basis with the others. Healing was dispensed equally to all of them. Jesus showed no bias and dealt a blow to any insinuation of the Samaritan's perceived inferior status. Indeed, Jesus was reflecting the true nature of God as a caring parent who loves and treats all his children equally.

Jesus exposed the hypocrisy and repulsiveness of racial prejudice. It must be remembered that in their life together the 10 lepers had already transcended their racial bigotry. Their common debilitating leprosy had made them vulnerable, but their common vulnerability helped them discover their common humanity, and their common humanity helped them overcome their inherited bigotry and xenophobia, and they became friends. Sadly, sometimes it takes a traumatic experience to wake people up and help them eradicate their racism. Racism is not something people are born with; it is something taught and nurtured.

Two millennia later, the questions Jesus raised concerning racism continue to haunt and challenge many communities around the world, including Israelis and Palestinians. The Palestinians today feel like the Samaritans of Jesus' time. They are discriminated against, their nationality and language are negated, and their right to their land is continuously undermined. They feel vulnerable before the military power of the Israeli army and the unruly extremist settlers. The discrimination against them is expressed in an oppressive Israeli occupation that violates their human and political rights and contravenes international law. The racism of Israel threatens and obstructs the way to justice and peace. Once racism is embedded in a community, it is difficult to uproot. Even when peace arrives, wholeness is slow to come, and scarred emotions and memories take a very long time to reconcile and heal. Racism is an epidemic that threatens the peace and well-being of a society. At times I wonder whether racism is a residue of primitive tribal instincts that we have not been able to overcome, expressing itself in oppressive and violent behavior against all those who are not members of our tribe, race, ethnicity, religion, color or sexual orientation. At the same time we celebrate whenever racism is vanquished through good education, authentic faith, true friendship and outgoing love. Good friendship can melt racial prejudice and make people cognizant of their God-given common humanity.

Jesus' core question can be a constant reminder to individuals and groups of their responsibility to strive against the racist epidemic. It is only then that peace based on justice and compassion can lead us to true healing, wholeness and reconciliation among our peoples.

Naim Ateek *is an Episcopal priest and the author of* Justice and Only Justice: A Palestinian Theology of Liberation. *He is the founder of the Sabeel Ecumenical Liberation Theology Center in Jerusalem.*

THOMAS ROSICA

"When the Son of Man comes, will he find faith on the earth?"

(LUKE 18:8)

—•••—

Ever since I can remember, this haunting question has puzzled me. Was it uttered with a sigh of hopelessness, despair or both?

The question follows a parable on prayer. In the Parable of the Persistent Widow, Jesus teaches the disciples the need for persistent prayer and the necessity of praying without losing heart, like the woman who insistently petitioned a dishonest judge for justice until she eventually obtained it. "Now shall not God bring about justice for His elect, who cry to Him day and night, and will He delay long over them? I tell you that He will bring about justice for them speedily," Jesus says, before asking his searing question.

Prayer means asking and seeking, knocking and waiting, boundless trust and infinite patience. As Old Testament scholar Walter Brueggemann has said, "Prayer is nagging God until God grants a petition for mercy and justice." Our own minds and hearts—and faith—are shaped by prayer. The prayer Jesus asks of us flies in the face of a world of quick fixes to complex problems.

Jesus' question about the faith he would find on earth is directed to believers—but what an astounding statement! If Jesus is telling us that when he comes back for his people, he may not be able to find faith among them, what exactly is the faith that he is talking about? Will he find a faith community that is putting its trust in Jesus and his word? A community intimately connected to him through prayer? Or will he find a church that has compromised and is relying on the worldly system to meet its needs and fulfill its desires?

Listen to what Pope Francis says about faith. In one of his more memorable daily homilies in the chapel of the Vatican guesthouse where he resides, given in October 2013, the Pope warned that without prayer, one abandons the faith and descends into ideology and moralism. "Woe to you, scholars of the law!" he said. "You have taken away the key of knowledge!" (Luke 11:53).

Pope Francis continued: "But how does it happen that a Christian falls into this attitude of keeping the key to the church in his pocket, with the door closed? ... The faith passes, so to speak, through a distiller and becomes ideology. And an ideology does not beckon people ... When a Christian becomes a disciple of the ideology, he has lost the faith: he is no longer a disciple of Jesus. The knowledge of Jesus is transformed into an ideological and also moralistic knowledge, because these close the door with many requirements."

Pope Francis speaks of faith as an exciting journey and a long history. He reminds us often in his daily homilies that believing in Jesus does not mean having absolute certainty and clarity about everything. Believing in Jesus is done on our knees, with humility and childlike simplicity. Believing in Jesus also means that there will be moments of terrifying desolation and profound consolation. And yet, believing in him means that we are never alone, and this knowledge sustains us for this arduous journey.

Faith in Jesus also gives us strength and boldness to let others know that Jesus has saved us and continues to save us. In Pope Francis' astounding interviews to the Jesuit publications shortly after his election, he reiterated the importance of the Church's unchanging doctrine, but he also said that "the church's moral edifice risks crumbling like a house of cards" if it is not balanced and put into proper perspective within the Church's timeless message of mercy, salvation and repentance. "The Gospel proposal must be simpler, deeper and more radiant," he says. "Moral behavior will flow from this proposal."

The cultivation of the faith is obviously God's work first, but it is also ours. What are we doing to make sure that the Christian Gospel is successfully passed on to the next generation? Pope John Paul II pointed out in 2003, "Many people are no longer able to integrate the Gospel message into their daily experience; living one's faith in Jesus becomes increasingly difficult in a social and cultural setting in which that faith is constantly challenged and threatened." How do we, as he said, bring "the Gospel of hope to all those who are far from the faith or who have abandoned the practice of Christianity"?

In the encyclical *Lumen Fidei* (the Light of Faith), drafted by Pope Benedict XVI and signed by Pope Francis, there is a beautiful section on the uniqueness of the light of faith:

"There is an urgent need, then, to see once again that faith is a light, for once the flame of faith dies out, all other lights begin to dim. The light of faith is unique, since it is capable of illuminating *every aspect* of human existence. A light this powerful cannot come from ourselves but from a more primordial source: in a word, it must come from God. Faith is born of an encounter with the living God who calls us and reveals his love, a love which precedes us and upon which we can lean for security and for building our lives."

St. John Paul II summed it up very well when he reminded us that Jesus' ultimate question about finding faith on earth is an open question which continues to reveal the height, the depth and the drama of one of the most serious challenges which our churches face today. Do we realize that we are bearers of this kindly light to a world filled with so much sadness, shadows and darkness? Do we really believe that we have a responsibility of passing on the faith to new generations?

Thomas Rosica *is a member of the Congregation of Priests of St. Basil and the CEO of Salt and Light Catholic Media Foundation and Television Network. He is also an English-language assistant to the Holy See Press Office at the Vatican.*

SHARON E. WATKINS

"For who is greater, the one who is at the table or the one who serves?"

(LUKE 22:27)

—•••—

It's not a trick question. The answer is obvious.

Eugene Peterson, in *The Message,* puts it this way: "Who would you rather be? The one who eats the dinner or the one who serves the dinner?"

Jesus continues, "You'd rather eat and be served, right?"

Obvious.

"But," says Jesus. "I have taken my place among you as the one who serves."

Oh, wait! It *is* a trick question. Following Jesus in God's realm means serving others—like Jesus did. This is a big revelation to the disciples gathered at the table.

Only this wasn't the first time Jesus had tried to make this point. One day, early in their time together, Jesus sat down with his little band of followers. He told them then exactly who would be blessed in the reign of God—those who are now poor, hungry, weeping; those who are hated, excluded and reviled because they follow Jesus. All these will have a place at the table in the Kingdom of God (Luke 6:20–26). In the Kingdom of God, expectations about place and status are turned upside down. The last are first. The servant is the greatest. All are welcome at the table.

Apparently, that first teaching did not take. Now, during what would be his final few days, when Jesus is on the verge of arrest, his followers break into a quarrel about rank among them when Jesus is gone. Perhaps it seems like an odd moment to bring up the subject.

The truth is, however, the question might have come to mind exactly because they were at table. Meals in Jesus' time were conducted with strict protocol. Everyone had a specific place, depending on their status relative to everyone else in the room. You knew exactly how you rated socially by who was seated on your right and on your left. Jesus had just warned them this was his last meal. They might, indeed, wonder about the seating chart at the next meal. Who would be in charge, and who would be chief of staff?

But Jesus said those were the wrong questions. Jesus told them they needed to focus on serving, not seating. In the realm of God, where love reigns, serving one another is the highest honor. The disciples found it hard to absorb the message.

It's a hard word to get across in the 21st century too—and apparently newsworthy.

When Pope Francis knelt at the feet of prisoners and took their feet in his hands to wash—*their* feet in his *hands*—it made international news. It was Pope Francis following the implication of Jesus' words to the disciples: "I have taken my place among you as the one who serves," and therefore you must serve too. Pope

Francis was on every news outlet that week—as one who serves.

Other people have caught our attention through their serving. Mother Teresa served among the poorest of the poor. Eboo Patel and his Interfaith Youth Core organize young adults to cross religious and cultural boundaries and unite through service. President Jimmy and Mrs. Rosalynn Carter have shown the way for thousands who serve by building houses for others through Habitat for Humanity.

It's newsworthy because not everyone would do it. And yet, surprisingly, serving others actually feels good.

My husband is the cook in our family. He finds joy in cooking a good meal for others. "When I cook, I want to eat last," he says. "I want to wait till everybody else has their meal. My joy is in their joy. It just makes me feel good to serve them."

There is something in our human nature that wants to reach out to others!

I see it in other cultures when I travel. In the Democratic Republic of Congo, people wait for hours to greet our plane. They welcome guests with singing and dancing. They bring gifts. One man walked an entire day through the tropical forest with a large jar of honey from his own bees—honey he wanted to give to us.

It makes people feel good to reach out to others. And yet, like so many things—going to the gym comes to mind—it feels good afterward. The challenge is getting started, making yourself get up and go.

Who is greater—the one who sits at table or the one who serves? In the end, it's not a trick question. The answer is that in God's Kingdom, the one who serves is greatest. And the good news is— our true human joy lies right there—in giving and in serving, in helping others flourish.

In my family, the birthday tradition is that following a celebratory meal together, the cake is brought to the table, candles blazing, and set before the birthday person. A song is sung, a wish made, candles blown out. We cheer. Then the birthday person—the one we are celebrating—the honored one—cuts the cake and serves—and shares the joy.

In my faith tradition there is also a table Christ's table. It reminds us of that very meal where Jesus told his followers, "I am among you as one who serves." At Christ's table we taste of bread and wine. We feast on the community formed there and the palpable presence of the love of God. We remember Jesus' question to his disciples, "Who is greater, the one who is at table, or the one who serves?" And we remember his answer: the one who serves.

Sharon E. Watkins *serves as the general minister and president of the Christian Church (Disciples of Christ) in the U.S. and Canada.*

"Judas, are you betraying the Son of Man with a kiss?"

(LUKE 22:48)

Does anyone want the moment of their worst decision to become the one thing people would have to say about them for the next 2,000 years? If we can learn anything from the life of Judas Iscariot it would be to never make critical, life-altering decisions on a bad day. Was Judas simply a betrayer, the disciple who sold out Jesus to the Romans for 30 pieces of silver? Was he an unsuspecting player in revisionist biblical history? Was he a participant in Jesus' own eschatological vision? Or did Judas make a bad decision that became a tragic legacy leading to his own suicide?

There is little known about Judas, but we do know he was born in Judaea, in a town called Kerioth. His parents were probably devout Jews understanding the importance of the name you give your child. They would have been familiar with the proverb that says, "A good name is rather to be chosen than great riches" (Proverbs 22:1). In many devout Jewish families, painstaking efforts were made to ensure the name given their son was in some way connected to his ultimate destiny. Judas' family chose a good name that had been held by one of the 12 sons of Jacob, and as such became the name of one of the tribes of Israel. They chose a name that had been held by one of the Maccabean heroes who had led a successful revolt for Israel centuries earlier. They chose a name that meant, literally, "Praise of God." There must have been pressure associated with a name like "Praise of God."

Children today are frequently given names like Mark, James, John, Matthew, Luke, Peter, Andrew and even Thaddeus, after one of the disciples. But no one names his or her child Judas. The irony—what once was a good name is today associated with the worst case of snitching in the history of religion. A good name, the name of one of the men closest to Jesus, ultimately became synonymous with the term *traitor,* and in any standard dictionary, Judas now means "a treacherous person."

Judas has another side not usually characterized in most biblical portrayals. What if Judas was a very close friend of Jesus who was asked by Jesus to betray him? And, what if this calculated betrayal paved the way for Jesus' prophetic mission to be fulfilled by facilitating the arrest of Jesus and his ultimate Crucifixion? This was the challenging scenario outlined in the 2nd century C.E. account of Judas' life discovered in a cave in the Egyptian desert in the 1970s and titled "The Gospel of Judas."

To compound Judas' story, the biblical Gospel writers themselves each give different reasons for Judas' betrayal. The writer of John positions Jesus' knowledgeable involvement of Judas as fulfilled prophecy. The writer of Mark has Judas betraying Jesus for no reason. The writer of Matthew refers to greed as the reason for the betrayal. The writer of Luke points to Satan entering Judas, causing him to betray his friend.

It is completely possible that the disciples needed a scoundrel to receive their angst, and the person closest to the leader is often the target. It is also plausible that Judas was the "beloved" friend of Jesus in that he was the one selected by Jesus to initiate the final series of events before the ultimate Crucifixion. Did Jesus choose Judas, or did Judas willfully betray his friend for some undisclosed reason? Clearly Judas was unable to defend his position because of his death by suicide, and every writer piled on the "betrayer" as the ultimate scapegoat.

The truth of the matter is, no one really knows what the impetus was for Judas' actions, but we do know that either failure, shame or remorse caused him to take his own life, subsequently killing the prospects of hope for reconciliation, restoration and the truth to ever manifest.

The real tragedy of this story is that Judas was obviously a trusted friend of Jesus who either made a poor decision or who followed Jesus' betrayal instructions to the letter and could not live with the implications of his actions and subsequently took his own life.

Suffering can and does visit people of all economic, social, ethnic and religious experiences, and we may never know what a person's genuine capacity for despair and ensuing breaking point may be. Often all it takes is one last thing when a person is already at the end of their proverbial rope. Suicide is complicated, brutal on family members, often connected to mental-health struggles, and it often leaves the victim's story to hypothesis and conjecture.

George Iles, an early 20th century Canadian actor and author, is attributed with the saying, "Hope is faith holding out its hand in the dark." The real challenge for the hopeless is seeing the hand of hope in the midst of darkness. Isolated and with multiple fingers of accusation pointing in his direction, Judas ran out of hope. Whether the recorded events were by his actions or a literary device, Judas became forever the one who betrayed Jesus.

What if we remembered Judas in love and not condemnation? If the account of Judas' life could be told from an outlook of love instead of contempt it would help the reader identify the *moments* of God's presence in the midst of life's challenges, the *methods* of God's redemption in the face of shame and the *message* of God's love in hostile environments. If we could be reminded of the value of life from the tragic story of Judas' death, we may also have fewer people killing themselves as a way to escape the sadness of aloneness, the shame of public ridicule and the sentence of a poor decision. We could hold out our hands in hope and learn to see others holding out their hands to us.

Rudy Rasmus *is the pastor of St. John's United Methodist Church in Houston and the author of* Love. Period.

"Why are you troubled?"

(LUKE 24:38)

Two objects cannot occupy the same space. Love and hate, truth and lies, the prophetic and the pathetic, faith and fear, certainty and doubt, cannot occupy the same space. For one to thrive, the other must be addressed.

Let us consider fear. Fear is the enemy of faith. Fear prompted Adam to hide in the garden, provoked Peter to deny Jesus and captivated the disciples of Christ to stand in unbelief as their resurrected Savior stood before them, just as he had promised. Fear prompts people to discriminate, embrace intolerance, hide in segregated communities and discard the fact that we are all, without exception, created in the *imago dei,* the image of God. Fear builds walls, silences truth, quenches love and dies in the proverbial desert of life without ever stepping into the promised land. For fear does nothing less than captivate, intimidate, destroy, bind and, above all, amplify the pathetic while quenching the prophetic.

Yet the most striking feature of fear lies in the following unfortunate reality: it always stands accompanied by none other than its persistent accomplice, doubt.

Approximately 2,000 years ago, Jesus addressed both fear and doubt. The resurrected Lord appears miraculously in a room where his once faithful followers gathered. His presence should have prompted arguably the greatest celebration of all. Yet instead of praising voices, Jesus encounters perplexed souls. Instead of unbridled faith, the Son of David finds himself in a room full of frightened faces and skeptical hearts.

Subsequently the Son of God proceeds in submitting a query that reverberates throughout his creation even to this day: "Why are you frightened?" he asked. "Why are your hearts filled with doubt?"

Jesus was asking, "Why do you permit fear and doubt to define you?" Just as Jesus appeared to his disciples after his death and resurrection for the purpose of redefining their lives, today, via the conduit of his Spirit, he continues to appear in the most difficult moments of our lives, not to condemn but to facilitate an environment where we can discover him while simultaneously discovering ourselves.

This simple truth revolutionized my life. As a Hispanic American raised in a region of our nation that suffered from cultural myopia, I sought definition. I yearned for a purpose that provided an antidote to my surroundings.

To a great degree, I too know what it feels like to be confined in the proverbial upper room waiting for clarity and asking whether my dream will survive today's uncertainty.

One evening when I was 14, I watched a Billy Graham special. His clarity and delivery stirred something inside. Subsequently on PBS, a Martin Luther King Jr. program aired highlighting his famous "I Have a Dream" speech. At that precise moment my purpose stood defined: live to reconcile Billy Graham's message with Martin Luther King Jr.'s march, live to marry sanctification with service, holiness with humility, righteousness with justice and truth with love.

That catalytic encounter provided spiritual corrective lenses to my myopia. On that day I understood that I am not defined by my surroundings, I am defined by God's Spirit inside of me. I recognized that I stand defined, not by my past failures, but rather by his eternal forgiveness; not by what I have been through but rather by where I am going, not by what others say about me but by God's purpose inside of me.

I arrived to the unshakable truth that I am not even defined by what I do for God. I am defined by what God already did for me. Jesus defines me; his love, mercy, grace, righteousness, joy, peace, sacrifice, atonement, Resurrection and Spirit define me. I am who "I Am" says that I am.

When Jesus appeared in that room 2,000 years ago, he did not seek the understanding of his disciples; he desired their trust. God is less interested in our understanding and more interested in our trust. Thus the question arises: Do we truly trust him? Do we truly believe his words, purpose and promise for our lives?

It's not to say that by trusting God we will never find ourselves face to face with the prophets of fear and unbelief. Quite the contrary. Both the actions and words of Jesus provide an unbridled assurance that at the end of the day, his peace will reign and his purpose will be done.

Armed with that commitment, we must proceed in confronting the very elements that exacerbate fear and increase doubt. When we know who we are in Christ. When we understand what we have, a Spirit of power, love and sound mind, then we can stand before the culprits of troubled hearts and unbelief to declare the following:

For every Pharaoh there will be a Moses, for every Goliath there will be a David, for every Nebuchadnezzar there will be a Daniel, for every Haman there will be an Esther, for every Herod there will be a Jesus, and for every devil that rises up against us there is a mightier God that rises up for us!

Jesus also provided an immediate solution for his disciples to overcome fear and doubt: touch me. "Look at my hands. Look at my feet. You can see that it's really me. Touch me and make sure that I am not a ghost, because ghosts don't have bodies, as you see that I do."

Touch me! In a world full of moral relativism, spiritual apathy, ecclesiastical lukewarmness, bigotry, discord, war, hatred, fear and unbelief, there exists good news; we can still touch God. We can touch God with our faith in him and our love toward our neighbors. We can still touch God by welcoming the stranger, feeding the hungry, clothing the naked and being light in the midst of darkness. We can still touch God by doing justice, loving mercy and walking humbly before him.

My prayer and hope resides in the expectation that future generations will say of us, "That was the generation that touched God! That was the generation that replaced fear with faith and unbelief with unbridled love and in doing so, they changed the world!"

Samuel Rodriguez Jr. *is the lead pastor of New Season Christian Worship Center in Sacramento, Calif., and president of the National Hispanic Christian Leadership Conference/CONELA, a Latino evangelical organization committed to serving more than 40,000 member USA churches and more than 100 million born-again Latino Christ followers globally.*

ARCHBISHOP JOSÉ H. GOMEZ

"What do you want?"

(JOHN 1:38)

—•••—

John the Baptist urged them to follow.

They were in Bethany, beyond the Jordan River, when John picked Jesus out of the crowd as he was walking by. John told them: This is the one we've been waiting for, the one the prophets taught us to hope for.

The two men took John's words to heart and immediately left to follow Jesus.

Now, Jesus turns and sees them. He asks: "What do you seek?"

He knows what they are looking for even before he asks. That's the way it is with Jesus. He doesn't ask questions to gather information. His questions are a mirror he holds up to us.

The question that Jesus asked those first disciples is the same one he puts to you and me, and to every man and woman in every time and place. What do *you* want? What are *you* looking for?

We are born with restless hearts, and his question cuts like a knife, makes our hearts burn with the questions we are born asking ourselves: What am I doing in this world? What happens when I die? How should I live? What path should I follow to find happiness and satisfaction? How can I be certain?

Jesus answers these questions simply. He turns to the two men and says: "Come and see." A command. An invitation. A promise.

We hear this story of encounter over and over in the pages of the Gospels.

Many who heard Jesus could not bring themselves to follow. There was the rich young man who grew sad when he realized he was not willing to give up his comforts. Others said they had too many things going on, too much work to do, family obligations. Maybe someday, they seemed to say.

But there were those who were looking for answers, for healing, for forgiveness. For them, these words—"Follow me, come and see"—became the word of life, the truth that set them free to live again.

Jesus taught that in God's creation there is not a sparrow that falls from the sky that God does not know about. He cares for all and for our smallest needs. Every hair on every head is numbered. Every child is born with a personal angel watching over in heaven.

In showing us the face of God, Jesus revealed that every human life is sacred and precious and has a purpose in God's loving plan for the world.

It was a radical message then. And it is a radical message now.

Sometimes I think this is the hardest Christian truth for people to accept. The universe is so vast—how can God possibly care for *me*? How can I be "somebody" to God when I'm living in this big, anonymous world where I am a nobody to almost everybody else?

What Jesus revealed, what his church continues to teach, is that our lives are not a casual fact, our existence not some random occurrence. Before the world began, when the earth was without form and void, when darkness was on the face of the deep—already then, God knew your name and mine and he had a plan for our lives.

"He chose us ... before the foundation of the world. He destined us in love to be his children ... according to the purpose of his will," St. Paul writes in the first lines of his letter to the Ephesians.

It is staggering to think about what that means. The God who created the sun and the moon, the stars and all the planets— this God wanted you to be born. More than that, he had his own personal reasons for wanting you to exist.

Our Father. This is not just the name of Jesus' most famous prayer. It is the reality that should change everything for us—our relationship with God and our relationships with others; how we see ourselves and how we understand our place in the cosmos.

Jesus is saying that before anything else—before we belong to any race, nationality, religion, political party or self-identity—we are children of God. And again and again in the Gospels, people were "astonished at his teaching."

His teaching should still astonish us.

What if we really believed that we are loved, that we are wanted, that we are needed? What if we really lived every day as if the Creator of the universe loves us with a parent's love? As if each person we meet is loved as we are and also has a part to play in the higher purposes of God's love?

Those first disciples in Bethany met Jesus late in the day. It was about 4 in the afternoon. They passed the night with Jesus. We don't know what they talked about. But the next morning when they set out, their life had new meaning and new direction.

They wanted to tell everyone—proclaim it from rooftops if they had to—that they had found what every human heart is longing for. They were using his words now: *Come and see!*

For all of us, the encounter with Jesus is not the destination, it's the beginning of the journey.

The call of Jesus has changed the lives of the saints who changed history—great figures like Francis of Assisi, Ignatius of Loyola, Teresa of Avila and Catherine of Siena; and in our day, St. John Paul II and Blessed Mother Teresa.

This call is still shaping lives every day. The lives of millions of ordinary people whom history will never remember; "unknown saints" who are changing this world one heart at a time—through the love and kindness they show to the people they live with, their friends, the people they work with; through their works of mercy and acts of justice in their communities and countries.

Since our encounter with Jesus, we now walk the pathways of this world with him, in the company of brothers and sisters who have also heard his voice and followed. We walk together as one family, staying close to Jesus and trying to live as he did—guided by his teachings and the example he gave us.

Each of us is playing the part he has given us in his mission—trying to create the kind of world that God intended for his children. A world where no one is a stranger, where everyone is welcomed and wanted and nobody is discarded or marginalized.

What did we want, and what were we looking for?

Like those first disciples, we too have found the answer in our seeking. We have come to see that it was always and only Jesus.

Archbishop José H. Gomez *leads the Archdiocese of Los Angeles, the largest Catholic diocese in the U.S. He writes at ArchbishopGomez.com.*

SPENCER REECE

"Woman, why do you involve me?"

(JOHN 2:4)

‑‑•••‑‑

You do not expect a priest to be formed by women. Until quite recently, it tended to be a masculine enterprise. But my formation has been marked by what women showed me. Sometimes directly, sometimes indirectly. I never imagined that the collar around my neck would be fastened with some confidence only after spending more than a year with a bunch of girls.

My career as a priest has been one of accidents. I never meant to go to Honduras and teach poetry to abandoned and abused girls at the only all-female orphanage in Honduras, a country of 180,000 orphans. I had never taught English as a first or second language, never put together an anthology, never spoken Spanish all day, never lived behind a wall with a bunch of girls. Never, never.

In 2010, when I was studying at Berkeley Divinity School, Yale, I went to do my clinical pastoral education at Hartford Hospital in Connecticut. Curiously, I did not *want* to go to Hartford. It was my last choice. A 1,000-bed hospital, where we had a helicopter that landed on the roof and an emergency room that was like a battle scene from the Tet Offensive: limbs, blood jets, screams. Often the ER saw victims of gang violence, and often these patients did not speak English. The amount of times I was paged by nurses to offer spiritual support only to stand there mute became ridiculous. I could not continue; I felt fraudulent. I called my bishop, a Cuban American, and said I could not take it anymore. I had to learn Spanish or else forget this whole song and dance with the collar and the black shirt and responding to "Father."

The bishop said, "I have just the place for you."

I said, "Where's that?"

He said, "San Pedro Sula, Honduras. There is an orphanage for girls there. Get a grant. Go in the summer. You will start learning Spanish."

I said, "Where is Honduras?"

In 2011, I spent two months at that orphanage—primarily in silence. I did not feel like I was contributing. Spanish was frustrating. I would stand like a telephone pole with the lines cut, a deaf and mute wooden thing in the middle of the courtyard, while the girls screamed. All around my feet were decapitated Barbie dolls, their exploded blond heads strewn about like dandelion blossoms postbloom. I was not a kid person. Hospice sounded better to me.

After two months of verbs and rain and lizards and electrical shortages, my bags were packed and I was ready to return to America. I could articulate little. But there is no doubt that the poverty I saw in one of the poorest Spanish-speaking countries in the western hemisphere was a part of me now: the beggars at the street corner, the prostitutes, the grit, the beans and rice had all seeped into my bones. What would I do with my witnessing? The girls' love was in me too, with the way they accepted me, hugged me. As someone with back-pew church attendance and a mild awkwardness with sharing the peace, I was entering the church with trepidation. The affirmation I received changed me utterly. What would I do with it?

During my last night there, I walked up to my apartment and saw that a young girl was waiting for me at the bottom of the stairs.

I said, "What are you doing here?"

Silence. She looked up at the stars. Over the 10-ft. wall someone was burning plastic. Palm fronds blew in the night breeze and sounded like a hand combing through files in a filing cabinet.

She said, "Don't forget us."

I paused. Haltingly, like an actor unsure of his lines, I said, "No, no, of course, I won't forget you." I went to my room. I looked at my luggage. And from that day forward I have been unable to get the girls out of my head. An unlikely road-to-Damascus moment. They needed advocates; that was clear for anyone to see. How could I honor her request? Maybe she said it to every gringo who passed through. But why was I standing in the middle of my room crying?

The press has perhaps unfairly dubbed San Pedro the "murder capital of the world," relying on statistics that were questionably reported. Certainly violence there exists, but I felt no more than I do in the U.S.

In 2013, I went to live in Honduras for one year as a priest and teacher, with a plan to put together an anthology of poems by the girls and invite a film crew to make a documentary about them. The day I left for my trip was the day of the Newtown, Conn., shooting—28 dead, mostly children. How quickly would they be forgotten? I had a cousin who was killed in the States in an unsolved murder, taken to a river after a bar fight and drowned. Everyone forgot him. No one should be forgotten.

And there I was that night, sitting at a table with 20 girls poised to tease me relentlessly; usually their game consisted of asking me who was my girlfriend. When I would point to one of them and say, "This one," that person would reject me with mock disdain. They all laughed at this. Mightily. Called me *chancho,* which means pig. This game went on for an entire year as the upper-grade girls wrote their poems. I think now they were showing me Christ's big banquet of love. Was there ever anyone who loved more intensely the more violence increased?

Close to the end of my time there, one girl, who had the home's most unspeakable story (she was found in a well with a rock around her neck, thrown down by her stepmother), told me that all those things that had kept me from church—feeling the loner, the outsider, odd, suicidal, unloved, different—made me a good priest. She ordained me once more.

Spencer Reece *is a poet and Episcopal priest. He lives and works in Madrid, where he is the secretary for the Bishop of the Spanish Episcopal Church.*

ROMA DOWNEY

"Do you not understand these things?"

(JOHN 3:10)

I believe that if people of faith were truly honest, they would admit that regardless of their belief system, there is an element of mystery that pervades our relationship with God. Intellect plays an important role in our spiritual journey, but a real relationship with God must also leave room for the sacred mystery. I believe that is part of what Jesus was teaching "Israel's teacher" in this text from the Gospel of John.

These words come from one of my favorite encounters of Jesus. He was visited at night by one of the leading religious leaders of his day. The man's name was Nicodemus. He was a Pharisee and a member of the Jewish Sanhedrin. It would have been hard to be more religious, in the traditional sense, than Nicodemus was. And yet we find him coming to Jesus to attempt to understand things that Jesus had obviously demonstrated but that Nicodemus could not understand. In his own words, Nicodemus says to Jesus, "Rabbi, we know you are a teacher who has come from God. For no one could perform the miraculous signs you are doing if God were not with him." In response, Jesus confronts Nicodemus with his need for a spiritual awakening that Jesus refers to as a second birth, a birth in the Spirit. And when Jesus continues to explain, he moves Nicodemus' thinking into the realm of the mysterious. "The wind blows wherever it pleases," he says. "You hear its sound, but you cannot tell where it comes from or where it is going. So it is with everyone born of the Spirit."

As a child, I grew up with a strong faith. I was raised Catholic in war-torn Northern Ireland. My husband Mark Burnett was raised Protestant in England. In many ways, we were an unlikely duo as we were from opposite sides of the divide. Yet love built a bridge of peace and reconciliation between us, and through our marriage God has worked in miraculous ways to make himself known. When we began to work on our miniseries *The Bible,* which we produced together for the History Channel, we spent hours studying the Bible, especially the life of Jesus, and couldn't have imagined how God would encourage us and reveal himself to us in mysterious ways as we shot the drama on location in Morocco.

One of the more obvious signs of God's presence came when we were shooting the scene from which these texts are taken. The Bible says only that Nicodemus came to Jesus at night, as he and his disciples were in Jerusalem for Passover. We set the scene up as if it had occurred around a campfire outside the city walls. When Jesus began speaking of the mystery of the work of the Holy Spirit, a strong breeze began to blow. As the wind began to blow the hair of our Jesus (Portuguese actor Diogo Morgado), without a beat he began to speak these very words: "The wind blows where it will." Chills ran down the spines of all the crew as we sensed that God had taken over the special effects of the scene. It was wild and it was mysterious and it was wonderful.

In ways we can hardly imagine, God works through mystery. He draws us to himself. He puts us in situations where he can make himself known in the depths of our being. I played an angel on the series *Touched by an Angel* for almost 10 years, and we used to say, "Coincidence is God's way of remaining anonymous."

God speaks to us without audible words. He demonstrates his love in amazing ways. He works in the daily routines of our lives, and he transcends those routines with times of mystery. He is God.

Roma Downey *is an Irish actor and the producer, with husband Mark Burnett,* of The Bible *and its sequel* A.D.: The Bible Continues *as well as* Son of God, The Dovekeepers, Ben-Hur *and* Unveiled.

ALEXIA SALVATIERRA

"Will you give me a drink?"

(JOHN 4:7)

—•••—

Women in the ancient Middle East usually came to draw water from the well in the early morning, the coolest part of the day. The Samaritan woman in John 4, however, comes to the well at noon— the hottest time of the day. Why?

We learn through her conversation with Jesus that she is a woman with a sexual history and status that would be considered shameful in her community. It's possible that she knows that she has to come at a time when the other women are not present to avoid their hard stares and cutting remarks. When she arrives at the well and she sees Jesus, she does not expect him to address her—it would have been surprising for any Jewish man to talk to any woman or Samaritan in a public place, and given her status, the last thing that this particular woman expects is for Jesus to ask her for a drink of water. She may have even assumed that this request was the first step toward a different kind of proposition. She doesn't seem to be entirely opposed to that possibility—her response to him is playful, possibly even flirtatious. His initial response also seems to be somewhat playful, but the conversation quickly deepens.

It must have been an amazing experience for her; Jesus is taking her seriously, talking to her as if she is capable of profound spiritual insight, listening to her words and truly paying attention to the person underneath and behind the words. He may not actually want a drink, but he does want something from her, something that is far deeper and more personal than the simple slice of her that men have craved in the past.

The story reminds me of a moment during a Christmas party years ago, when I was co-coordinating a homeless drop-in center. One of our mentally ill homeless regulars, "Debbie," came in to the party weeping. She had spent the day sitting in front of a department store in the cold. She had been watching people walking in and out all day buying presents for their families and friends. The deepest cause of her tears was not the painful truth that no one would be buying her a present but rather that she did not have any capacity to give a present to anyone else. She shared through gasping sobs that it was so terrible not to have anything to give that anyone wanted.

One of our deepest core human needs is to be valued. The greatest proof of our value is when people want what we have to give.

Sadly, the value of our contribution is not always recognized. In December 2005, the Sensenbrenner Bill passed the House of Representatives. If the legislative proposal had passed the Senate, it would have become a felony to be an undocumented immigrant or to help an undocumented immigrant. I knew a number of undocumented immigrants at the time whose reaction was absolute anguish. They were invariably people who had been working quietly for many years, raising American-citizen children—coaching Little League and volunteering at their churches—and suddenly their contributions seemed to be invisible. Suddenly it seemed like the nation didn't even see, let alone value, all that they had to give.

Hebrews 13:2 reads, "Do not neglect to show hospitality to strangers, for by doing that some have entertained angels without knowing it." The Koine Greek word that we translate as "angel" does not merely refer to celestial beings—it refers to any messenger of God sent to bring a blessing.

The Rev. René Molina, pastor of Iglesia de Restauración in Los Angeles, came to this country without proper immigration documentation. When he came to his church, it had 10 members. It now has more than 4,000. Many of the members of his church have seen their lives change in wonderful ways as a result of their faith. They have left behind destructive habits, built strong families, worked hard at their jobs, helped their neighbors, volunteered for community service—and even at times engaged in community development and community organizing. By any measure, René and his wife Hanelory have been "angels," bringing blessing to South Los Angeles, contributing morally and spiritually as well as practically to our city.

I believe that Jesus asks us all to "give him a drink." He values our gifts and welcomes our contributions, whoever we may be. He looks at us and sees an infinitely precious creation of God, underneath and behind our words, valuable in a way that all of our brokenness and sin cannot diminish. This is part of what we mean when we speak about the grace of God. God's grace is found not just in his many gifts to us but also in his valuing of us and our gifts. As children learn to love by being loved, this experience of the grace of God is designed to make us similarly grace-full in our relationships with each other. We "give Jesus a drink" by receiving the "drinks" that we are given by the people around us "gracefully" with joy and gratitude.

From 2000 to 2002, the Los Angeles convention and visitors' bureau and the mayor's volunteer bureau commissioned artists to produce several hundred sculptures of angels and distribute them around the city. They were ultimately auctioned off to benefit charities. I remember during that time that I often found myself looking around for angels. It was always such a delight to find one.

What will it take to see the unlikely angels in our midst? And when we see them, what will it take to ask them to give us a drink?

Alexia Salvatierra *is a Lutheran pastor and the founder of the Faith-Rooted Organizing UnNetwork. She coordinates the Welcoming Congregations/ Guardian Angels Network for the Southwest California Synod of the Evangelical Lutheran Church in America and is a co-author of* Faith-Rooted Organizing: Mobilizing the Church in Service to the World.

ECUMENICAL PATRIARCH BARTHOLOMEW

"Do you want to be healed?"

(JOHN 5:6, ESV)

—•••—

When we read in the Christian Scriptures about Christ as a physician and healer, most of us imagine a miracle worker or magician, someone who might be invoked to intervene in order to solve problems. We envision a deus ex machina—a mechanical or metaphysical figure who reaches out of the heavens to alleviate tragedies and dispel controversies.

Such a perception, however, contradicts the image portrayed in the Gospels. In almost every healing miracle, Jesus first seeks to elicit acknowledgment of the circumstances that require change or demand remedy. Despite his express mission to "bring good news to the poor, proclaim release to the captives, recover the sight of the blind and liberate the oppressed" (Luke 4:18), he persistently underlines the prerequisite of "longing" and "desire" for the gift of "mending" or "healing."

Who could possibly not yearn or thirst for healing? Christ's question "Do you want to be healed?" applies to the personal as well as the public challenges that go to the core of our relationship with God, others and ourselves. Who has not prayed for a child to be cured, for a friend's survival of cancer or for recovery from traumatic abuse? Christ's words in John 5:6 are addressed to a paralyzed man, who patiently and persistently awaited heavenly healing beside a pool in Bethesda for 38 years. The healing challenge in the public sphere proves equally daunting. Who would not dream of a world where peace and justice prevail, poverty and suffering are overcome, and the earth's resources are fairly shared?

Missing from these challenges is a frequently overlooked aspect of Christ's healing miracles. What is of paramount importance in Christ's ministry of miracles is not simply the conclusion or culmination of healing the suffering, but rather his eagerness and determination to convince those whom he encounters that he is feeling their suffering.

Are we likewise able to feel the suffering in our world? Are we able to make compassionate choices for ourselves and for others? In our personal lives, do we accept responsibility for our anger and jealousy, our greed and arrogance, our addiction and anxiety? For such recognition is the only way that these can be healed. In the public arena, are we prepared to demonstrate our preferences and voice our choices? Do we dare to declare our priorities and struggle for policies on energy and food, war and injustice, global warming and biodiversity? After all, "where our treasure is, there will our heart also be" (Matthew 6:21).

When we are healed, Christ might urge us to "go and sin no more" (John 8:11). Nevertheless, another force continues to impel and pull us in directions contrary to our natural inclination and irreconcilable with our personal choice. St. Paul explains: "In my inmost self, I delight in God's law; but I see within me another law at war with the law of my mind, making me captive to the law of sin" (Romans 7:22–23). The reality is that we live in a world of spiritual tension and irreconcilable choices.

But do we at least *want* to be healed? In the face of global terrorism and political instability, are we committed to seeking common ground that unites Christians, Muslims and Jews, as well as people of every color and culture? Do we labor to create bridges wherever we encounter division and dissension? Do we favor dialogue whenever we confront prejudice and intolerance? Can we discern the face of our brother and sister—ultimately, the image and likeness of God—in our enemy as in the extremist, in the fundamentalist as in the fanatic?

Do we at least want to be healed? In the face of global warming and climate change, are we willing—or do we resist the responsibility—to adopt simpler lives and live more frugally? Can we truly believe that a century of pumping oil-fired pollution into the atmosphere will have no ramifications on our world and no consequences for our children? The Prophet Isaiah predicted: "They look, but choose not to see; they listen, but choose not to hear" (6:9–10). The world is a gift from God, offered for healing and sharing; it does not exist for exploitation or appropriation. The way we relate to God cannot be separated from the way we respect other people or the way we treat our planet.

So do we choose to heal? Because if not, we are denying our very nature as human beings. If we choose not to care, then we are no longer indifferent onlookers; we are in fact active aggressors. If we do not allay the pain of others, then we are contributing to the suffering of our world. If we do not choose to heal the suffering around us, then ultimately we do not "want to be healed." Like Christ, then, it is our vocation and obligation to seek out the oppressed and to discern the consequences of our actions. If we do not work for the welfare of our world, then we do not genuinely desire to be well. In our efforts for healing and reconciliation, we must ask ourselves some difficult questions about lifestyles and habits. Just how prepared are we to sacrifice our excessive life-styles—that is to say, when will we learn to say, "Enough!"—in order for others to enjoy the basic right to survive?

We are all surrounded by people in need, who are suffering. There are so many people around us without hope, who require healing. Do we see them? Do we choose to respond to them? Are we a healing presence and the healing hands of Christ? If we really want to be healed, then we must be prepared to accept a new way of living; we must be reintegrated into a way of sacrificial living; we must be restored into a way of compassionate living. Indeed, we must be willing to bring that healing and wholeness, that reconcil-iation and newness, into our surrounding society and planet. For this is surely the ultimate healing that we should want: the healing and transformation of the whole world.

His All-Holiness Ecumenical Patriarch Bartholomew *is the Archbishop of Constantinople—New Rome and spiritual leader of the Orthodox churches worldwide. In 1997, he was awarded the Gold Medal of the U.S. Congress for advancing interfaith dialogue and environmental awareness.*

SARA MILES

"Does this offend you?"

(JOHN 6:61)

---•••---

When Jesus shockingly tells his friends to eat his flesh and drink his blood, he uses a very particular verb. He doesn't invite them to dine or to savor. He asks his horrified disciples to "munch" or "gnaw" on his meat, using graphic language that describes noisy, animal eating. It's hungry eating: urgent, even desperate, as if life depends on it.

His words are *meant* to be offensive.

Jesus' invitation to eat him, to abide in his life, to in fact become him is so invasive and weird that many of the disciples run away, scandalized. Even those who stay, like Peter, term it a "hard teaching" and "intolerable." I'm no less freaked out than any of them were. But what else can we do? To whom, as the disciples say, shall we go? Where can anyone escape the offensive truth of what it means to be human?

For one thing, human reproduction is bizarre. I remember when I was a new mother, and a friend asked me what it was like to have a baby. Apparently, I was too tired to be delicate. "Uh," I told her, "well, it grows inside of you, and it comes out of you, and then it eats you."

Children are the gift of life, new life. But what that means is a hard teaching: life is given through sex and pain, eating and bodily fluids.

It's easy to turn childbirth into a greeting card, breast-feeding into a kind of pastel fantasy and the relationship between parents and children into romance, glossing over the offensive physical details. But each of us is somebody's child. This means that you grew inside a woman, you came out of her and you drank from her body to live. You became part of her, and she became part of you. Her genetic quirks, her bone-marrow cells, her habits are still in you, in ways that can feel as uncontrollable as the moment you were pushed out from between her legs in a great rush of blood.

This is intolerable.

You are somebody's child. A man helped make you. He put part of his body inside someone else's body and became part of yours. The shape of his hands, the color of his eyes, his desires—he still lives in you, in the code of your cells, in particularities that stay with you all your years.

This is intolerable.

But where else can we go? Being human and receiving the gift of life involves great, great love. It also involves pain, blood and the specific demands of bearing difficult relationships.

And so when Jesus declares that he is the gift of eternal life and offers to feed us with his own body—of course it's a hard teaching. The life Jesus gives to all people on the Cross, just like the life our parents give us, is not romantic. Jesus' gift requires seeing the reality of the incarnation, of birth and death, in ways that often seem too crude, too violent, too offensive to accept. And Jesus' gift demands that we stay in a relationship with God, and with other people, no matter how much we want to run away.

My father died unexpectedly 20 years ago, and some days I can't bear not having him here to wrap my arms around. And yet the ways in which he still feels present to me, alive to me, are often strangely physical. Sometimes I glance down and see my dad's hands at the end of my arms—the same crooked pinkie fingers, the same thin wrists and wide palms. I remember looking at his hands when I was tiny and playing with them; I also remember the first time I noticed that my daughter had inherited the same bent pinkies. I catch myself talking loudly and sounding exactly like him, or stroking my daughter's hair the way he used to stroke mine.

None of this makes me not miss my father; it makes me miss him terribly. But he still seems as much a part of me, body and soul, as ever; maybe even more. He abides in my flesh, and I've come to trust that he abides in God too. Not because I have some special spiritual knowledge or a particularly great faith, but because I see how the real lives of my father, of me, of my daughter—how all our lives are bound up with God's life, which doesn't end.

Does this offend you? That humans are made out of meat and that we're suffused with a longing spirit we can't entirely understand? That we are each the child of a mother and father, made through love and suffering, and that we're God's children too, made through love and suffering? That we are penetrated by and inside each other, connected to and bearing with each other, that we receive life from and give life to other humans through our literal flesh and blood? That we die and receive new life through God's own flesh and blood, Jesus?

These are hard words, the disciples say. But where else can we go? We have to be born, eat, drink and die right here on earth in intimate communion with our mothers, fathers—all the people around us, whom we didn't choose. We have to argue with and put our hope in God, whom we didn't choose.

But God chose us. And God, through Jesus, keeps choosing our bodies to abide in, to carry the gift of life, eternally.

Sara Miles *is the director of ministry at St. Gregory of Nyssa Episcopal Church in San Francisco and founder of The Food Pantry. She is the author of* Jesus Freak: Feeding Healing Raising the Dead, Take This Bread: A Radical Conversion *and* City of God: Faith in the Streets.

NEICHELLE R. GUIDRY

"You do not want to leave too, do you?"

(JOHN 6:67)

—•••—

I recall an experience I had in high school, which is, of course, the most socially exhausting four years of one's entire life. So much pressure to fit in and to conform. Such devastating realities for those who never find a clique or a crew in which to belong. My freshman year, I had a group of girlfriends who gave me a sense of sisterhood and "coolness." With them, I bought into the myth of color blindness; I never saw the difference between their whiteness and my blackness.

Until I saw it.

Sophomore year, all of them suddenly turned on me for no apparent reason. True story. And when I began to probe, supposedly their turning had something to do with my "looks," which struck me as odd because at some point, I was cute enough to hang out with them. So as I took note of the new girls they had let into the crew, the only difference that existed between our "looks" was due to our difference in ethnicities. To this day, I don't have a memory of a more painful rejection, and I've learned that despite the time that has lapsed, some things will always sting simply because they are true stories.

Jesus' question in this text strikes me for a number of reasons. First, I'm struck by the context. Jesus is having a moment of extremely high visibility. He'd just fed the hungry multitude with two fish and five loaves of bread. They were anxious to learn more about him, even to the point of crossing the sea over to Capernaum to find him the day after he miraculously supplied their sustenance. They wanted him.

To be wanted is a human desire. So human is this desire that it closely mirrors God's own desire to be wanted by humankind. And often, in the quest to become wanted, it is tempting to present an inauthentic portrayal of who we are. We each have an instinct to "give the people what they want" to ensure that we remain wanted.

Which is exactly what Jesus *didn't* do. Upon their arrival, he began telling them the truth about themselves: "you are looking for me, not because you saw signs, but because you ate your fill of loaves." Jesus seemed very clear that the crowd was more interested in what he could do for them than in who he was and what it really meant to be in his life. And rather than shrinking from his truth, he took their presence as an opportunity to be very transparent with his newfound following. Because no one wants to be wanted for merely utilitarian purposes. Not even Jesus.

And the multitude leaves. He was great while they were benefiting from his ministry, but when they learned that Jesus required reciprocity, the crowd dispersed. His teaching was too hard. He was too much to handle. But then he turns to the Twelve, his hand-selected inner circle of those he may have called his friends. He asks them, "Now that you know who I am and what I require, do you want to leave, too?"

I'm also struck by the way that Jesus tells the truth about himself. At this point in his life, he's in his early 30s, and like me has had his share of pain from rejection for being his unique and wonderful self. But it seems as if the one thing that he wouldn't do was compromise who he was just to be accepted. Jesus exemplifies a profound self-security that made it possible for him to let some people walk away.

Telling the hard truths about who we are and our expectations of others should be basic forms of social self-care. But it can be difficult and risky to the heart that is born to live in communion. In this story, Jesus demonstrates that the only way to approach such tasks is with intentionality and utter honesty. He shows that in all relationships, we teach others how to love and accept us. And yet, despite this discomfort, Jesus saw the value in the vulnerability that it takes to fight for some relationships.

There are certain people who find their way into the intimate spaces of our hearts and lives. What they think about us, how they treat us and where we stand with them actually matter to us. We trust their opinion. We seek their guidance. They have a refreshing presence. And despite our greatest efforts to be "strong," we don't want them to leave our lives. These are the few whom we "choose," as Jesus chose the Twelve.

With this question, Jesus conveys that in all relationships, the choice for acceptance and vulnerability must be mutual. There must be a shared commitment to the journey of becoming friends and to the work of being a good friend.

I've heard some popular theologians preach about how we should "let them walk" when people want to leave our lives. How we shouldn't resist it when people want to walk away. Ultimately, this is what I had to do with my "friends" in high school. However,

Jesus' question challenges this idea—with certain people. The question warns us of the fact that some people *will leave*. Therefore, this question ultimately strikes me because it also reveals the possibility that some people will stay.

And even if only a few remain out of the masses, we are doing well. When I think of my chosen few (all two of them), I am humbled by the years we've put in and the hard conversations we've had. They have witnessed the contradictions in my life, and yet they have remained. They've restored what was broken when my so-called friends in high school walked away. And in the face of vulnerability, they give me courage to say the words that are necessary for love and growth to occur. Just like Jesus did with this question.

And this is the blessing that is bestowed when your chosen few also choose you. Because when all is said and done, we really don't need fans and followers. We need *friends*.

Neichelle R. Guidry *is the liaison to worship and arts ministries at Trinity United Church of Christ in Chicago. She is the founder of shepreaches, a professional-development organization that aims to support and inspire black millennial women in ministry.*

AMY BUTLER

"Woman, where are they? Has no one condemned you?"

(JOHN 8:10)

—•••—

Compare the Gospel of John to the other three Gospels and you'll be struck by a few noticeable differences. For instance, in place of a birth story we get a beautiful theological discourse on words and light and God coming to live among us before the author of John jumps right into a narrative that runs from the early days of Jesus' ministries through the terror of his Crucifixion.

Along the way, John treats us to many stories of Jesus interacting with all kinds of people who come across his path—stories that don't all appear in the other Gospels but each of which sheds a little more light on who Jesus was and what he was busy trying to do. One such story is Jesus' encounter with the woman caught in adultery.

One day Jesus was busy teaching in the town square when local leaders brought a woman accused of adultery right to the front of the large gathered crowd. There was no question about whether or not she was guilty of the adultery in question—that seems clear, but the writer of John's Gospel neglects to mention the other party involved in the adultery charge.

Maybe nobody cared about the man involved; it was and still often is women who bear the consequences for such indiscretions.

Or maybe this gauntlet-throwing incident wasn't really about adultery after all.

This scene with the woman—and the questions Jesus poses to her—comes at a critical point in Jesus' ministry. Jesus and the message he preached had begun to garner widespread curiosity that was increasingly leaning toward sweeping public adulation.

As the town leaders treated the woman to a public ritual of humiliation, it became clear that underneath the facade of moral outrage was a mounting panic about Jesus' growing acclaim. Public opinion was shifting, the temple leaders could feel it, and they were determined to bring the full force of institutional religion to bear on the situation.

In front of everyone, the woman's accusers made a case for her death, loud and insistent, determined to prove to the crowd that Jesus didn't have the courage to follow clear-cut temple laws. The text says they were looking for a charge to bring against Jesus, using rules meant to create healthy community as weapons to discredit this one they found so threatening. Jesus surely knew what they were doing, and he managed to ignore them long enough to collect his thoughts. Finally, he spoke up. He invited anyone among them to pick up a stone, grip it tightly in a fist and throw it hard at the woman—anyone, that is, who themselves had never sinned.

Brilliant.

As Jesus' words settled over the crowd, I imagine you could have heard a pin drop. I think, had I been standing there watching, my own curiosity might have shifted to shame, or at least chagrin. I surely would have tried to be discreet as I dropped the rock I'd clutched in my own fist. The self-righteous indignation fueling my outrage would have instantly cooled: the woman may have been guilty, but who isn't guilty of some failure of judgment, some selfish act, some hurtful choice?

The text says that one by one the woman's accusers turned and slunk away.

It was then that Jesus asked his questions: "Woman, where are they? Has no one condemned you?"—questions that, we all know, were not really questions. They were wry commentary, surely delivered deadpan with a straight face.

The questions Jesus voices here don't illumine for us Jesus' opinion about adultery; they're not even meant to illustrate his considerable political skill. These questions were raised to remind the crowd and remind us: Jesus had little tolerance for hypocrisy; Jesus chose persons over politics every time; Jesus encountered people in pain and invited them to life-giving grace, again and again.

In Jesus' voicing these questions, I suspect, he invited the crowd to let out a collective sigh of relief. Nobody except Jesus had the guts to say out loud what everybody was thinking: we all make mistakes. Every one of us lives with the challenge and opportunity of our flawed humanity.

The gift Jesus gave the crowd that day, and the gift we modern readers receive as we hear Jesus' questions for our own lives, is this: Jesus is not afraid to tell the truth about what it means to be human. And every encounter we have with God should be filled with that kind of truth telling, covered with grace upon grace upon grace.

Modern culture has come to see institutional religion formed in the name of Jesus as a gleeful group of temple leaders who gather to pass judgment on people who just don't measure up. We religious types would do well to remember that Jesus is always soundly on the other side of those exchanges, naming the truth and insisting that we always err on the side of grace.

Amy Butler *is the senior minister at The Riverside Church in New York City. She writes and speaks on the topics of faith, community and the future of the church.*

RICHARD RODRIGUEZ

"What shall I say? 'Father, save me from this hour'?"

(JOHN 12:27)

—•••—

Stupid! How did I imagine I would get my mother's wheelchair through this crowd? *Where are we going?* she asks for the 11th time. *Is papa coming?* Papa's right behind us. Papa will relish seeing a dead man sit up and swallow bread.

Jesus is on his way to Jerusalem for the Passover. He has stopped at the house of Lazarus and Mary and Martha, who are arranging a dinner for him. It is one of the strangest dinner parties on record—a zombie dinner—for Jesus has only recently raised Lazarus from the dead. People who lately filled the house as mourners now fill the house with rejoicing. There are people squatting in the corners, people leaning upon the walls, people in the courtyard, people taking turns at both windows. Wild Mary produces a bowl of nard; she proceeds to rub it between the toes of Jesus, then dries his feet with her hair! Fragrance of nard fills the courtyard.

If Jesus feeds us magic sardines for lunch, we look to him for dinner. If he cures the blind man in one village, the blind woman in the next village wants to see too. Crowds enlarge into mobs, trailing the miracle worker. Jesus must hide from the crowd of believers as often as from his enemies. And if his piety is not real, then he is working tricks. If his works are not tricks, then what are they? It is too wonderful to imagine!

"Nothing can save us that is possible"—W.H. Auden's line. Indeed, one of the earliest lessons we learn about life on earth is death. The baby bird on the sidewalk. Clouds. Absence. Death makes mothers weep at weddings. Death makes grandparents rest- less at christenings. "Poor baby"—my father's blessing. "We who must die demand a miracle"—Auden's line.

Passover celebrates an exemption from death for God's chosen people. Long ago in Egypt, the angel of death passed by the doors of the Israelites that were marked with blood. Those Israelites who were spared that night would die in time, but not before they were rescued from Egypt, not before they were confirmed before nations as God's chosen. The raising of Lazarus was similarly an exemption, a sign for the crowd, though Lazarus too would die.

The Gospels are unbelievable. The evangelists, the writers of Gospels, are far from the documentarians we might wish them to be. They are, nevertheless, mindful to record who was present on occasions they recognized as important and incredible. The writ- ers of the Gospels are insistent. *We saw. We heard. We preserve what happened to us in order that you may believe.* But the interference of centu- ries surrounds the person of Jesus. Jesus can scarcely complete an utterance or a gesture without it being taken up by the whisperers and made to conform to messianic prophecy.

The chosen apostles of Jesus did not seem to know or care much about scriptural overtones or undertones. They were men with ready hands; they were followers of a man who said, simply,

Follow me. The phrase that most often recurs in the Gospels with reference to the apostles is: *They did not understand.* The apostles are constantly being told by Jesus that they will comprehend his meaning only after his death. We read the Gospels backward, therefore—in the light of the Resurrection and not as the apostles lived their lives. The apostles groused and their stomachs growled and they walked their legs off. The apostles loved Jesus immoderately.

The chief priests in Jerusalem have agreed among themselves to have Jesus arrested if he enters the city during the feast of Passover. A crowd has formed outside the gate of Jerusalem, waving palms as if for a conquering hero. Jesus mounts the back of a donkey, not like a Roman, more like a bumpkin fool.

I am sure some in the crowd hope for an arrest. Others in the crowd await a medicine man who will fix their knees or peel the cobwebs from their eyes. Some think he is the one foretold.

As Jesus approaches the city, John's narrative abruptly shifts its scene and its time frame. We read that Philip, a disciple from Galilee, who has come to the city for the festival, has been approached by "some Greeks" who want to meet Jesus. Philip searches the crowd for Andrew, finds him, and the two then approach Jesus to convey the request. This odd intrusion into the fateful progress lends verisimilitude—nothing has more loose ends than real life.

So: Do you want to meet some Greeks? The occasion of the question rather than the question itself elicits from Jesus a rehearsal of one of his perennial agrarian tropes:

Now the hour has come for the son of man to be glorified. In all truth I tell you, unless a wheat grain falls to the earth and dies, it remains only a single grain ...

If I were filming the scene, I would do exactly as the writer of John has done; I would fade the sounds of the crowd. I would lock the camera's focus on the downcast face of the man on the donkey. I would employ voice-over to indicate that the speech is in the nature of an interior monologue and the question it raises rhetorical:

> *Now, my soul is troubled. What shall I say: Father, save me from this hour? No, it was for this very reason that I came to this hour. Father, glorify your name!*

Immediately, there is an answering assertion from within or without nature. *I have glorified it, and again I will glorify it.*

The noise of the crowd is once again present in the moment. The crowd has heard something. Of course the crowd is confused and at odds with itself about what it has heard. Some say it is a crack of thunder. Others say an angel is speaking to Jesus.

Jesus answers the crowd: *It was not for my sake that this voice came, but for yours.*

The crowd reforms itself into a dramatic chorus at this point, contesting the image Jesus employs to describe his apotheosis— *When I am lifted up from the earth, I shall draw all people to myself.* The pedantic whisperer intrudes upon the reader: *By these words, he indicated the kind of death he would die.* But the crowd isn't buying it. The crowd says: The law has taught us that the Christ will remain forever, so where do you get this *the son of man must be lifted up* business? Who is this son of man?

This is the same crowd, this is the same question, this is the same misunderstanding that has puzzled Jesus for 2,000 years.

My father is deaf. He cannot make out the crowd's objection. But he sees clearly enough that Jesus is a dead man. *Let's go,* he says.

My mother is tired. Messiah or no messiah, she wants to go home.

Richard Rodriguez *is the author of numerous works, including* Darling: A Spiritual Autobiography *and* Hunger of Memory: The Education of Richard Rodriguez.

AMY GRANT

"Do you understand what I have done for you?"

(JOHN 13:12)

—•••—

One recent Saturday, I found myself with an unexpected stretch of solitude at the end of a glorious sunlit winter day. I drove to the place where my husband Vince and I were married, the same hillside where my mother's ashes are buried. I took a long walk in the woods and built a roaring campfire just as the sun was setting.

Coyotes began yipping and howling in the distance. Their eerie cries escalated to a frenzy ... then fell silent.

I wondered what they were doing.

I wondered what I was doing.

Sometimes I come here just to be.

Several years ago, I was sitting in this same spot as an afternoon storm approached. The wind was loud and the sky was yellow-green. Down the hill the air exploded with dirt and tree limbs. A small twister must have touched down.

I was a little nervous that day but not afraid.

Being out in nature feels like being a guest in God's house. Even if you are not talking to him, you know he's there. The sense of God's presence in the stillness that I find here is the reason I keep coming back.

I felt the same thing as a child on Sunday mornings, Sunday evenings and Wednesday nights, when we sang in harmony at the Church of Christ. The hymns brought the feeling of his presence.

Sitting beside the crackling fire, I welcomed the stillness. It had been a busy time, and I had been looking forward to a night like this.

As I studied the stars and stared into the blackness beyond, I felt a presence in the vastness of the universe and a tightening in my chest. I used to imagine being in outer space, untethered and drifting helplessly unchecked. I had that sensation now.

"Our Father who art in Heaven …"

Saying the words out loud removed all feeling of separation.

The hair on the back of my neck stood on end; a shiver ran through me. And my heart raced.

The feeling was bone-chilling and unexpected, as if I had lowered my face into the surface of a wave and found myself staring into the eye of a whale.

I recognized God's presence.

"Do you know what I have done for you?" Jesus asked his disciples after he had washed their feet, on the night he would be betrayed.

Do you know what I have done for you?

I can barely wrap my mind around the edge of that thought, the way my eyes can see only a tiny piece of the universe.

As the Gospel writer said, "No one has ever seen God, but God the One and Only, who is at the Father's side, has made Him known."

Amy Grant *is a Grammy Award winner whose career spans more than 30 years, from her roots in gospel music to becoming a pop star, songwriter, television personality and philanthropist.*

WM. PAUL YOUNG

"Will you really lay down your life for me?"

(JOHN 13:38)

---•••---

The way the week began, none of us would have predicted how it ended. The events of the days preceding our auspicious entry into Jerusalem were like a storm gathering together massive apocalyptic clouds. Each of us could feel it, and we were willingly carried along by its rising swell.

Jesus, raising his friend Lazarus from the dead, was now like a massive trumpet blast awakening the twin terrors of religion and politics as well as many hopeful hearts. It rippled out from Bethany like a wind-driven inferno.

We knew the tide was changing and began jostling for places and positions that would soon be assigned to those who had been most faithful, namely the 12, especially me. It was infuriating when James and John got their mother involved in the debate over who would sit at Jesus' right hand in the coming kingdom, the politics of preference, probably because the rest of us hadn't thought of it first.

As much as Jesus resisted the surge, it appeared to be too much even for him, and we were glad of that and thought it best.

Somewhere in all the activity and excitement, the reasons we first followed him dissipated; his simple invitations, the kindness and laughter and word-stories that spilled from his lips like a living river stirring places in our hearts that seemed long dead.

Instead, we now lusted for attention, recognition and the embrace of any and every prophetic anticipation that might justify our violence against the enemy. God was on our side and this moment our destiny. The ages would honor us as men of might and valor, so we strode confidently into the city, accepting the adoration of the crowds.

I've heard stories about the conquerors of Rome returning to their city—magnificent parades surrounded by the adulation of worship and the powers bestowing gifts of nobility, wealth and position. And now, with God's help, we were going to overthrow Rome itself and reap the benefits.

And then he turned his back on all of this. He walked away.

I was utterly crushed and undone, furious and fuming, internally a mass of accusations and despair. What was he thinking? I left everything to follow him to end with nothing but broken dreams and no consideration or appreciation for what I have given up? For more than three years I had wandered with this gang of misfits, mocked and ridiculed. I gave up generations of security and risked my family relationships, for what? For nothing!

Why in that moment King David came to mind, I don't know. Perhaps because we were standing in his city, close to Mount Zion. What would he have done? He spent years wrongfully pursued and somehow stayed a man after God's heart. David, who blistered the ears of God with his rage and vengeance—we all knew his songs. In my imagination I was David telling Jesus how I felt.

"Jesus, I don't know if I trust you anymore. I thought I loved you and you loved me, but I don't think that's true. You are walking away from everything I hoped, as if I don't matter. You've taken years from my life and left me, what, a handful of dust and dreams, embarrassment and fear. This is your fault. I am so disappointed and so furious that I could ..."

Did I tell him? Did I speak of what was in my heart? No. Instead, I buried it as deep inside as I could dig and then tried not to let it show. I am not a king, after all, only a stupid fisherman. At the time it didn't cross my mind that David was a shepherd.

Over years I have learned that concealing such things never turns the ashes cold. Any passing wind ignites these embers into flame and burns anyone nearby. I was adrift in a tangle of heaving emotions underneath a placid sea, caught between the need to be important to this man and the desire to run away or die.

Everyone was irritable, our words tipped with thorns to cut and hurt. I wasn't about to raise another finger to do another thing, and then he picked up the basin and one by one began to wash our feet. A simple act of kindness, a gesture of grace cut through all of our self-pity and offered an invitation to honesty. I didn't take it. Instead, I smothered the opportunity under a humble-sounding but self-serving command. I bluntly told him not to touch me.

Another invitation and another chance to come clean, but instead I acted self-righteous and pious, almost as if it were his privilege to wash my feet. Then he talks of a betrayal, and it felt like all eyes were turned in my direction. I deflected such glances with my best nonverbal accusations, but in my heart I wondered, Is Jesus talking about me?

Once more I refused to be authentic and tell him of my heart. Instead I declared my boldness and my willingness to die on his behalf. I desperately wanted him to put his arm around me, to turn and face the others and hear him say, "Here is a true friend and brother, a man I can count on. To have such a gift is worth more than countless stars. Peter is someone I can depend on, an example to you all."

He didn't. A sad smile before he responded, "Really? Will you really lay down your life for me?" He let it hang, this final invitation, and then added, "You won't betray me only once, but three times."

It was never my intention to deny Jesus. I would have sworn I was incapable of such a deadly act. When we hide, we often act from the pits of undisclosed emotion rather than choosing what or who is important. For me, it took only one question from a child—"You aren't one of this man's disciples too, are you?"—but her little insinuation tore open all my darkness, which then exploded. Cursing, I swore an ugly oath, that I never even knew him.

Wm. Paul Young *is the author of* The Shack, Cross Roads *and* Eve.

> # "My Father's house has many rooms; if that were not so, would I have told you that I am going there to prepare a place for you?"
>
> **(JOHN 14:2)**

"Oh, I still can't believe that you've loved me for eternity. And what's so marvelous to me is that I finally get ... to love you back." —Jamie Grace, *"To Love You Back"*

I remember the day my daddy told me the King of the World loved me. I had heard him preach it from the pulpit, been encouraged by the songs my mom would sing and even heard my older sister Morgan talk about our Savior from time to time, but it was nothing like the day I realized the invitation was also extended to me.

My dad told me that even though our world was broken, there was still hope, and that hope was because God sent Jesus to die for our sins so we could live in heaven with him someday. Jesus also rose from the dead after three days of being buried and he would be in heaven as well. My mind was blown, my heart was full and at 7 years old I asked my dad to help me pray a prayer to ask Jesus into my heart so that I could be with him in heaven but also live a life that pleased him while on earth.

One of the most compelling aspects of Christianity is the invitation. It is truly an invitation extended to *all* people. One does not have to be born into the right family or able to make the appropriate accommodations. The invitation extends to everyone for eternal life with the Creator of the world ... with the King!

In John 14:2 Jesus says, "My Father's house has many rooms; if that were not so, would I have told you that I am going there to prepare a place for you?" In this passage Jesus was speaking to his disciples—his followers—and it may seem natural to presume that the invitation he speaks of to his Father's house, to heaven, is merely for the 12 in his presence at the time. However, we have been given an invitation as well. We have the opportunity to become followers—disciples of Jesus Christ—and to accept the accommodations made for us in heaven.

I cannot think of another King who has invited his children to live with him in a place like heaven. I cannot think of another King who would send his son to die for our sins so that the price for heaven would be free. The only reason I could think that he would choose to do something so extravagant, so out of the ordinary, so marvelous? *Love.*

As it is so blatantly put in John 3:16, "For God so loved the world that He gave His one and only Son, that whoever believes in Him shall not perish but have eternal life," God did all of this for love.

Often it seems like all everyone is looking for is love. I'm a 23-year-old college grad with a full-time job and a house—I think it's time for me to fall in love! *Smile.* But that kind of love has to have perfect timing, as we like to say. Even so, before I can understand that kind of love, before any of us can search for or accept the love of someone else or even before we can truly love ourselves, we should know that there is a love that has been there all along. We should invest in a love that doesn't need to wait for the guy and the girl standing in line at the coffee shop flirting over whose order should be placed first. This isn't the kind of love that requires a conversation to find out if both parties are still invested in the relationship.

This love has a standing invitation from love himself asking for a relationship with the ones he loves the most: us.

When I sat down to write the song "To Love You Back" with friends Dave Wyatt and Gabe Patillo, I found myself quiet for most of the session. If I had lyrics to contribute I would, but there was a calm in the studio that was not comparable to our normal sessions. Dave and Gabe are both in TobyMac's band DiverseCity and have been like big brothers to me since I started working with them when I was 19. Now that I'm 23, their families feel like my own and we often laugh more than we work. Not this day.

I walked into the studio to hear Dave and Gabe working on the concept for the chorus, and as the day went on we continued to expand on the idea and connect with the realization that *the* King, *the* Creator, has loved *us*—for eternity. It was emotional and over-whelming in the best way as we sat there writing a song thanking the Lord for all he has done for us. He started loving us before our parents were around, before our grandparents dreamed of their future generations ... He has always loved us! And now that we are here on this earth, we finally get the chance, the privilege, to love him back.

Prior to affirming the invitation to his disciples, Jesus had a few instructions to make known. He says to them, "Don't get lost in despair; believe in God, and keep on believing in Me." He never tells them that life on earth will be easy or simple; he actually tells them not to get lost in despair, indicating that they may feel hopeless at times. As a follower of Christ, I can say that I have felt hopeless at times. Since I was in middle school, I have been facing the struggles of having Tourette syndrome, but I am reminded through Jesus' words not to become consumed or lost in that despair. He reminds us to keep our faith in God, and in him, and assures that in his Father's house, there *is* room for all.

I anxiously await the day I get to join my Father in heaven. It will be a day when pain, fear, heartache, frustration, disappointment and sickness come to an end. But until that day, I will choose to live a life that represents the Father who chooses to love me more than I deserve to be loved. With his love, I will sing, write and preach, every chance that I get, to make sure I am doing my part in sharing an invitation that is truly extended to all.

Jamie Grace *is a singer-songwriter from Atlanta. She received a Grammy nomination and won the 2012 Dove Award for New Artist of the Year.*

CHRIS TOMLIN

"Who is it you want?"

(JOHN 18:4, 7)

----•••----

If I could travel back in time to witness a defining moment in the life of Jesus Christ, I'd go straight to his arrest as depicted in John 18:4–7. It remains one of my favorite Scriptures, especially verses 5 and 6. There, Jesus stands up to his enemies—and embraces a dark fate ahead—in a startling show of inner peace and outward power that boils down to three words:

"I am he."

Let's set the scene. We see Judas the betrayer, accompanied by a garrison of Roman soldiers. Here they come, marching with the chief priests and Pharisees who view Jesus as a threat. Judas has just betrayed his best friend. And Jesus has just returned from the Garden of Gethsemane, where he sweat blood that he'll later pour out on the Cross.

For me, it would be a time to run away or put up a misguided struggle against my captors. But Jesus knows this is the moment he's been born for. He steps forward and utters a seeming formality to seal the deal of his capture: "Who is it you want?"

"Jesus of Nazareth," *they* reply—meaning not just one man but many.

Jesus meets their three words with three of his own: "I am he."

The nuances here are subtle yet definite cases of "blink and you'll miss it" (not that the burly warriors did). The New International Version of the Bible puts the question this way: "Who is it you want?" Is Jesus Public Enemy No. 1 on the ancient equivalent of a WANTED poster? Or is he the one those arresting him unknowingly *want* to fill the deepest longing within—that not even a pantheon of gods can satisfy?

And taken on its face, Jesus' reply could simply equate to "Yes, it's me, you've got the right guy." But consider what happens next. The Roman troops find their swords and shields worth scrap. They topple like toy soldiers, their faces kissing the dirt. What an amazing scene.

Keep in mind that these armed men in service to a mighty empire were trained to protect its interests, to confront violent offenders and resistant forces at every turn. Yet Jesus brandishes a power that they'd never reckoned with. They had no idea whom they were up against. They had to answer the question: "Who is it you want?" The answer to them is obvious: Jesus of Nazareth. What happens next is not: They fall flat in an instant. You have to wonder what they thought just an instant before—some version of "We are the soldiers, we have the weapons, we have the authority here."

What authority? It had to be embarrassing for them. Awkward. They had to pick themselves up as though bested by a single schoolyard bully. But there's the person they've come to lead away, just standing there and offering no resistance.

As in so many previous standoffs with Pharisees and those who'd trap him, Jesus reverses the situation to make an unexpected point. And this point pierces as sharp as a rain of spears.

A few chapters earlier in John 8:58, a very similar declaration
sets the Crucifixion drama in motion. The Pharisees grill Jesus
about his divine authority, and Jesus answers, "Before Abraham
was born, I am!" In response, the religious authorities attempt to
stone him.

Yet in John 18, without so much as drawing a dagger or shooting a sneer, Jesus levels the mighty. With three words. Search the
Bible from Genesis to Revelation and you'll fail to find a shorter
three-word sentence than "I am he." *It is just five letters long in a vast
number of translations.*

But you will also discover that it's not the first time in Scripture that such a simple statement of identity has carried so much
blinding force. Think of Moses hiding his face from the burning
bush where God reveals his mystery and majesty: "I am who I am."

Moses was charged with the difficult task of speaking truth to
imperial power. Here, Jesus willingly submits to it. How heartbreaking. He knew thorns would be jammed into his head. That
he'd get beaten beyond recognition. That his beloved Peter, when
asked if he was a disciple, would deny him with an entirely opposite, cowardly reply of three words: "I am not."

Then: Jesus foresaw that a guilty person would go free, while
he as an innocent would be crucified. A crowd likely filled with
followers who once adored him would turn with hatred and
malice. Furthermore: He knew the next hours of his life were literally going to be hell on earth. If we could ever use the phrase in the
right way, all hell was about to break loose. He knew it was coming
at him and that later he would tumble into hell's horrific depths.

Who among us wouldn't shrink back in utter fear and anxiety?
Not even a saint, I'd suppose. This explains why I feel that in this
Gospel moment I can once again recognize Jesus as both man and

God. His world was rife with trickster prophets and false agents of the divine. But here, Jesus shows he's not just another religious leader causing trouble or inciting a riot against the government. He was altogether different, and John 18:4–7 is a poignant punctuation to the narrative of his ministry.

We've gone back in time; now, let's venture back to the present. After two millennia, Jesus' answer still resonates with the questions so many of us nurse regarding our identities. The power we lack often intimidates us, and so we may seek it anywhere and everywhere. We stand for hours in long lines to buy high-tech gadgets that turn to landfill fodder in a few short years. We look to entertainers, pop culture and big-budget films for words to live by. We seek constant distraction and diversion on screens—even while they bombard us with ads that invoke "spirit," "soul" and "truth."

Yet the issue of who we are never goes away, whether we consciously inquire after it or not.

Now: Picture yourself planted in the face of trouble, torture and certain death. This would represent the ultimate crucible crushing you or me into powerlessness.

How amazing that Jesus could proclaim with certainty and serenity, a paradox of divine calm and conquering force: "I am he."

Chris Tomlin *is a Grammy Award–winning singer-songwriter and recording artist. He leads worship at Passion City Church in Atlanta and travels the world singing his worship songs, which have been translated into numerous languages. He actively supports the END IT Movement and CURE International.*

"Shall I not drink the cup the Father has given me?"

(JOHN 18:11)

-•••-

There is a time that I go back over in my memory often, now that I find myself writing about fathers and sons again, and watching my own sons grow into (and struggle with) becoming boys who will soon be young men.

It is Good Friday in early 1972. I am 9, and that makes my father 48. Our whole family is in a pew at church, and I am looking up at him as we stand for the Passion of St. John. The man's head of hair is like iron approaching gray, his salt-and-pepper beard close-cropped to his chin. The angular nose and cheekbones seem the distance of a long climb from where I am. And his eyes are closed. He is tired in the middle of the day. *No,* I think, *he is listening.*

It is a play of sorts, the Passion, and we, the congregation, are the crowd. But first (like any man who must struggle with himself before the rest of the world) there is the intimacy of Jesus praying in the garden. His disciples are there, tired and scared (my mother never failing to remind us—John, Thomas, Andrew and Matthew—of the presence of our namesakes), and then we are startled awake. Soldiers, betrayal, violence (a severed ear), and the salvific question posed for all of us gathered to pray: *Shall I not drink the cup my father has given me?*

I look back up at him. He opens his eyes, shifts his frame, puts his hand on my shoulder, not to say, "It won't be much longer," but to press me to pay attention to the words, the question, to remind me that this is what we do on Good Friday, remember suffering. "C'mon, you can do this for the Lord," he whispers.

What is this? I wonder. Understand sacrifice? See that we are part of the play? Drink the cup? But what son can drink, I ask myself now, until he understands what it is his father has given him?

He was 3 when his father died in a Wilkes-Barre, Pa., mine collapse. My grandmother was pregnant with her fifth child, and they sent her husband home in a box. So my father never had a father, only older brothers. They stuck together, worked together and fought for one another, fought anyone threatening to disrupt that family. All three were in the Pacific theater in the war, and all three came back and got on with the task of having families of their own.

We were a family of nine in the small town of Dallas, Pa. Seven kids growing up in a small house on the hill where my mother grew up. We heard a lot of stories about sacrifice and faith in those days, and I suppose that's part of the reason I gravitated toward religious life in my 20s and entered the Jesuit order with my heart set on being ordained a priest. That formation—eight years for which I am, to this day, still grateful—offered its own kind of sacrifice and faith, but in time I found that life more lonely than life-giving, and it was an agonizing decision to realize that this was not the cup for me. Could I not take it? When I told my parents that I had decided to leave the order and that I was scared, it was my father who put his hand on my shoulder and said, "C'mon, I'll make you a drink." And it was like I had been brought back to life.

He died in 2004 at the age of 80, two years before I published my first book, a year and a half before my first child was born. I often think that he would have loved the curiosity and spirit of my two sons, and surely the same in my daughter (as was his grandfatherly wont). And when I wonder what he—the dutiful father—would have thought about the fact that my wife is the one who works full time and I am the stay-at-home parent who writes, I try to imagine how his thoughts played out as he prayed on that Good Friday, what anxieties he as a father no doubt weighed. State budget cuts in a bad economy and the job he (a social worker) might lose. His eldest son's student deferment expiring, the boy's draft number low. The station wagon he bought used in need of repairs. Some deeper anxiety about what he'd dreamed of becoming and what he had become. And what if the Lord took this father of seven without warning?

Most Gethsemanes, I realize now, are gardens entered in ordinary time, and fathers, regardless of their jobs, share a vocation to tend. In that alone, my cup is no different from his. My 7-year-old son once blithely called me lazy. When I asked him why, he said that I didn't work like the other dads did. I stayed home. Cradling a child who is sick and crying at 3 in the morning, or doing laundry, shopping, shuttling to and from activities and doctors at all hours of the day, I think, *Will I ever write another book again?* Will I become anything close to what I dreamed of becoming? Then I think of my father, a man whose gift to me was never having placed an obstacle in my way, and I realize that I get only one shot at this.

No one will let me say, "Wait."

So I sneak an hour or two of writing in the early morning, alone in my room with words, then put that pen down as the house wakes and turn to the ordinary cup I've been given, having been taught from the beginning that it is an extraordinary thing to raise. Not to write a good sentence but to be a good father. And that becomes the only thing for which, in all seasons now, I pray.

Andrew Krivák's *novel* The Sojourn *was a 2011 National Book Award finalist.*

GENE LUEN YANG

"Why question me?"

(JOHN 18:21)

Hello!

I'm cartoonist *Gene Luen Yang.*

The other day, a friend said to me,

I feel like you're always *this close* to becoming an *atheist.*

Maybe he's right. I'm a practicing *Roman Catholic,* but every so often, I go through an intense period of *questioning.*

In the Gospel of John, shortly after *Christ* is arrested, he's brought before the authorities. When they ask him about his teachings, he replies,

Why question me?

But *how* does he say it?

Is he *indignant?*
Why question me?
How dare you?!

Frightened?
Why question me?
Leave me alone!

Calmly confident?
Why question me?
Come at me, bro.

I guess what I'm *really* asking is, does Christ *want* to be questioned?

I have to believe that he *does.* In the same passage, he tells his questioners,

Ask those who heard me.

In other words, *ask more questions.*

And that's exactly what I do. During those periods of *doubt,* I ask the folks around me who've experienced Christ, who've *heard him.* Sometimes they give me a reading list. Other times they just listen.

But always, they remind me that I am one of them, that I, too, have heard him.

Gene Luen Yang's *2006 book* American Born Chinese *was the first graphic novel to be nominated for a National Book Award. He writes the monthly* Superman *comics series from DC Comics.*

KEITH AND KRISTYN GETTY

"Woman, why are you weeping? Who is it you are looking for?"

(JOHN 20:15)

The psalmist in the Old Testament sings to God, "You keep track of all my sorrows. You have collected all my tears in Your bottle. You have recorded each one in Your book" (Psalm 56:8, NLT). In traditional Jewish culture, Psalms would often be read while visiting the graves of loved ones. These songs express many things about God, and often, as in this case, the lyrics find comfort in a personal God who is full of compassion and close to us in our suffering. So close he not only sees our tears but records and keeps them.

Mary's tears are also quite literally recorded here in the book of John. We read that Mary is crying by the tomb where Jesus had been laid, grieving his death and now the disappearance of his body. Her story can be followed through the Gospel accounts—she had been forgiven much and so loved much, and now the loss was too much.

Here, Christ finds her where she is. She is not a blurred face in a crowd; she is not hidden away behind a wall of those with some superior access to him; she is not left on her own. He sees her, sees her weeping. He speaks to her, asks her who she is looking for. Surrounded by the tombs of a grave site, they aren't strange questions. But they are questions he knows the answers to. He embodies the answers. They are asked for her individual understanding, not his. They reveal much about the personal relationship of Christ with his followers and our knowing who he is. The angels had also asked just a few verses before, "Why are you crying?" His followers had been informed to some level about all that would happen to him. Yet even after the angel's proclamation, Mary was continuing to think of the Lord as dead and did not recognize him.

She represents something for each of us as we too, at times, are blinded by tears and wrestle with the brokenness of life. However, there was no longer a need to weep these particular tears. "Weep you no more, sad fountains," the old folk song says, but in this case the lost one is not sleeping; He was dead and now is alive! By Christ's question, Mary was to learn his fuller identity and who she was actually looking for—the risen and not just crucified Lord. The question moves the story along from Good Friday to Easter Sunday. It lifts her from a downward spiral of hopeless grief to the high plains of hope beside the Savior.

It is interesting that in this particular context, the emphasis is not on *"what" are you looking for* but *"who."* It's personal. It's relational. Christianity makes several specific claims about the person of Jesus Christ. Of particular note for this part of the story is the deep-rooted conviction of the Lordship of Christ over all of life and knowing him as friend and King (for example, Philippians 3:8–9).

"See Mary weeping, 'Where is He laid?'/ As in sorrow she turns from the empty tomb/ Hears a voice speaking, calling her name/ It's the master, the Lord raised to life again/ The voice that spans the years/ Speaking life, stirring hope, bringing peace to us/ Will sound till He appears/ For He lives, Christ is risen from the dead"
—*Keith Getty and Stuart Townend, "See What a Morning"*

For us in the 21st century, the questions asked to Mary still speak. For at the heart of the human experience is the shared, seemingly inescapable enemy of death within us and all around us. Every generation longs and works for a way to outwit it, to conquer it, to outlive it, to find a Messiah. But in every moment around the world, there are many tears that fall on the cold stone of a grave and are left to dry without the hope of life. Who is it that we are really looking for? The Bible teaches our answer is in knowing him.

God gives himself. He himself has tasted the bitter tears of death so that ultimately we will not have to. Though we do not physically see him, all who honestly seek him will find him. Mary knew him not by his face but by how he called her name. Others recognized him through the unfolding of God's salvation plan explained through all of Scripture (Luke 24:13–35). The God who defeated death offers his nail-scarred hands to catch our tears and bring life to body and soul. The Book of Revelation says one day he will return and "He will wipe away every tear from their eyes, and death shall be no more, neither shall there be mourning, nor crying, nor pain anymore, for the former things have passed away" (Revelation 21:4 ESV).

God promises that the struggles that may still linger, the stings of sin and the sorrows that may yet weigh on his followers will not cause us to despair but will find their full hope, complete relief and perfect answer when Christ returns for those who recognize and know him as the one they had been looking for.

"Where doubt and darkness once had been/ They saw Him and their hearts believed/ But blessed are those who have not seen/ Yet, sing Hallelujah

The power that raised Him from the grave/ Now works in us to powerfully save/ He frees our hearts to live His grace/ Go tell of His goodness"
—Keith Getty, Kristyn Getty and Ed Cash, "Christ Is Risen, He Is Risen Indeed"

Keith and Kristyn Getty *are hymn writers and performing artists from Northern Ireland. Perhaps best known for "In Christ Alone" (penned by Keith and Stuart Townend and recorded by Keith and Kristyn), they are creating a catalog of songs teaching Christian doctrine and crossing traditional and contemporary music genres.*

MAKOTO FUJIMURA

"Friends, haven't you any fish?"

(JOHN 21:5)

I call this passage in the Gospel of John "the post-Resurrection breakfast." Behind Jesus' deceptively simple question lies the reality of the Resurrection, an invitation to layers and layers of probing and mystery. Peter and the other disciples are back at their jobs as fishermen after the death of their leader. They are now in survival mode, threatened both by the religious authorities who want to arrest them for blasphemy and by Roman authorities who consider them insurrectionists. The disciples are trying to stay quiet, despite hearing rumors of the resurrected Jesus. The tomb is empty; the women have excitedly said, "Come see for yourselves." Peter runs to the tomb and confirms with his own eyes that it is empty—but he does not meet the Risen Christ.

Peter goes back to doing what he knows best: back in the boat, casting a net, confused and acting as if nothing has happened in the past three years, years that turned him upside down.

Jesus knows their futility; he is the one who instructed them to cast their net on the other side of the boat. Peter's memory is awakened to when he first encountered the Son of God on the shore of the same lake. Then too Peter could not *see*. As a fisherman, to see a school of fish is his profession; but there is a type of abundance that he cannot see, not yet.

But now the disciples listen to the Stranger's voice, and the net is full again.

Peter says, "It is the Lord!" An awakened memory leads to a recognition. A response to that voice leads to an invitation to reconciliation. The last time Jesus' eyes met Peter's was right after Peter had denied him three times. The shriek of the rooster crowing must have reverberated in Peter's ears too.

The resurrected Jesus must have seemed an apparition to the disciples. As T.S. Eliot put it in his *Four Quartets,* they "but heard, half-heard, in the stillness/ Between two waves of the sea." On the road to Emmaus, they could not even recognize him until Jesus supped with them and broke bread. A common meal was the entry point for new perception, for new reality to open up. Like a Dalí painting, we just think what we are seeing is surreal, and something extradimensional, but what this passage suggests is that such extradimensionality is already flowing through our time and space. Every artist, every intuition, taps into such a greater reality.

In this already apparent reality, the flesh enters yet again, and the resurrected Jesus is fully present, both in body and in spirit. He has already started a fire on the beach and laid fish upon the coals; he waits with cooked fish. It is a quiet, ordinary reintroduction. Why did Jesus not reintroduce himself to Peter by exhibiting grand power, again walking on water? Or in a private, solemn meeting where they could speak of Peter's denial? What a way to reintroduce himself, not with rolling thunderclouds but by cooking breakfast on the beach! Jesus, in a typical gesture of abundance and even humor, asks the disciples to bring their catch and invites them all to a special post-Resurrection breakfast.

When I was asked a few years back to illumine *the Four Holy Gospels* by Crossway Books for the 400th anniversary of the King James Bible, Chapter 21 of the Gospel of John was one of the last pages I illumined. For some reason, this image of the fish by the beach became central to my John illuminations, so the first page of the John chapters has a fish illumined, a branzino—a type of fish that I imagine the disciples might have caught that morning.

But next to the words of John 25:5, I also depict another fish— this time a troutlike fish that is rising up in the margin of the page.

I thought about the fish that Jesus ate with Peter. What happened to that fish? Since there is no death in "life after life after death"—Bishop N.T. Wright's wonderful phrase to describe post-Resurrection reality—fish too, I reason, must be resurrected.

Some say that such "resurrection" is one's memory of the disciples' desire to speak of Christ, to continue to remember him. To me, the Resurrection is a physical imposition, not merely a psychological recognition. Christ's sacred reality invaded ours, embedded in the abundant physical reality. The Resurrection is a new generative paradigm, full of the aroma of Christ, that replaces the old limited-resource reality. Our limited minds and perceptions cannot *see* yet the fullness of that reality. The net of the disciples is full, but the net does not break. Both material reality and the supernatural reality of God hold all things together. Christ's resurrected presence is both, and as C.S. Lewis noted, in God's domain every blade of grass is weighty, filled with the weight of God's glory.

There is a sense in which at every moment since the Resurrection and the ascension, we have been in the presence of the resurrected reality. All artists sense this, or should. Wendell Berry challenges us to "practice resurrection." Heaven merges with earth, and we can experience, through our senses, something that angels cannot. We are invited to our own post-Resurrection breakfast, lunch and dinner. Would we, in supping the sacrifices offered through bread and wine, and fish, discover a taste of the feast to come?

Makoto Fujimura *is an artist and speaker and the author of* Culture Care: Reconnecting With Beauty for Our Common Life. *He was a presidential appointee to the National Council on the Arts from 2003 to 2009 and was one of the first artists to paint live onstage at Carnegie Hall.*

J. ROSS WAGNER

"Simon, son of John, do you love me?"

(JOHN 21:17)

---•••---

It is early morning. A small fishing boat lies a hundred yards offshore, its silent occupants numb with exhaustion. Simon Peter and his friends have labored all night but caught nothing. Now, in the first light of dawn, a voice calls from the shore. "Children, you have no fish, have you? Cast the net to the right side of the boat, and you will find some." The net that had come up empty all night long suddenly teems with fish. A moment of joyful recognition—"It is the Lord!"—and Peter plunges headlong into the lake. He swims to meet Jesus while his companions follow in the boat, dragging the heavy net behind them. When the tired men reach the shore, they find a small fire burning, with fish and bread already baking on its glowing coals. Jesus has made them breakfast. As once he fed the 5,000 by the lakeside, so now he feeds the dear friends whom he had loved to the uttermost by laying down his life for them on a Roman cross. This, John the evangelist tells us, is now the third time Jesus has shown himself to the disciples after rising from the dead.

After the meal, Jesus turns to Simon Peter. "Simon, son of

John," he asks, "do you love me more than these?" Though he has spoken about love throughout John's Gospel, only here at the very end of the narrative does Jesus pose the decisive question, *"Do you love me?"* Without hesitation, Peter answers: "Yes, Lord; you know that I love you." Gently, insistently, Jesus repeats the question a second and a third time: "Simon, son of John, do you love me?" All at once, Peter understands. The memories come flooding back: Jesus' midnight interrogation in the house of the high priest; the charcoal fire in the courtyard; the persistent questioning by suspicious bystanders; Peter's frightened denial of any connection with Jesus—not once but three times; his shameful abandonment of a friend to face torture and death alone.

Yet even as grief begins to well up inside him once more, Peter perceives in Jesus' thrice-repeated question the tenacity of a love stronger than death. Jesus, who willingly laid down his life, has taken it up again, for he shares the life of the Father who loves him. The grave cannot separate Jesus from those he loves; neither can Peter's faithlessness. In sorrow and in hope, Peter appeals to the one who knows him better than he has dared to know himself. "Lord, you know everything; you know that I love you."

In declaring his love for Jesus, Peter finds himself summoned to follow his master in the way of self-sacrificing love. Three times Peter affirms his love; three times Jesus replies: "Feed my lambs. Tend my sheep. Feed my sheep." Like the Good Shepherd who guides him, Peter too will one day lay down his life for those he loves. "When you grow old," Jesus prophesies, "you will stretch out your hands, and someone else will gird you and take you where you do not wish to go." The cruciform death that Jesus foresees for his disciple will be but the culmination of a life like Jesus'—a life poured out in devotion to God through loving service to others.

Jesus joins love of God to love of neighbor in an indissoluble bond. "Those who love me," Jesus says, "will keep my word; and my Father will love them, and we will come to them and make our home with them." To keep Jesus' word, and so to share in the life and love of God, requires nothing less than taking up the Cross and following Jesus in the way of self-giving love. "This is my commandment, that you love one another as I have loved you. No one has greater love than this, to lay down one's life for one's friends."

"Do you love me?" Two millennia after his encounter with Simon Peter on the lakeshore, the risen Jesus continues to confront would-be followers with this decisive question. Those who answer as Peter did will find themselves caught up in the everlasting embrace of divine love. They too will hear the glad summons that sends them forth and empowers them to spend themselves in love for their neighbors: "Feed my lambs. Tend my sheep. Feed my sheep."

J. Ross Wagner *is a professor of the New Testament at Duke Divinity School. His research centers on the interpretation of sacred texts in ancient Jewish and Christian communities. He is the author of* Reading the Sealed Book.

ROB BELL

"If I want him to remain alive until I return, what is that to you?"

(JOHN 21:22)

—•••—

The question, as they often do, comes at breakfast. It's not long after Jesus' Resurrection, and he's hungry, because, as we all know, you burn a ton of calories rising from the dead. He's there on the beach, grilling some fish and talking with his disciples, asking one of them, a caffeinated fella named Peter, if Peter loves him. Peter is adamant about his love for Jesus, but after the question is repeated the third time Peter realizes that this interaction is about something else. It's about Jesus essentially saying to Peter, I know you betrayed me three times, but now I forgive you and I've got something for you to do. I want you to take care of my followers ...

It's a beautiful, sacred moment between the two of them, charged with love and grace, but Peter misses the significance of it. He's distracted, looking over his shoulder, wondering about another of Jesus' disciples, one named John. Peter asks Jesus, What about him?

Jesus has just given Peter a path, a calling, work to do in the world, but all Peter can think about is John's path. Jesus responds to his question, If I want him to remain alive until I return, what is that to you?

I love this question. It's one of my favorite lines in the Bible. I love that Jesus answers a question with a question. I love that Jesus is really, really funny here. I love how strange and surreal it is, with a backstory involving rivalry and rumors and running races. There is profound, timeless wisdom for each one of us right here in this question that Jesus asks: What is that to you?

First, then, a little backstory.

In the Resurrection account in John's Gospel, Mary comes to Jesus' tomb, sees that the stone has been removed and runs to tell Simon Peter and the other disciple, the one whom Jesus loved.

Wait—let's stop right there. Because this is the Gospel of John, right? John is the one telling the story. And in this story John is telling he refers to Simon Peter and another disciple who is the one whom Jesus loved.

Who is he talking about? Himself! Classic. He describes himself as the one Jesus loved. As opposed to, you know, the other ones.

(By the way, there's a whole world of scholarship surrounding when the first four Gospels were written, the general agreement being that the Gospel of John was written significantly later than the other three. You can find massive volumes dedicated to explaining why this is so with extraordinarily detailed technical language. My theory is a bit simpler: John's Gospel comes later because he had to wait for the others to die, knowing that if they read his they'd be hacked off to say the least ... What? You're the disciple Jesus loved?!! You narcissistic, brownnosing, always-have-to sit-next-to-the-Messiah-when-we-go-out ...)

Back to the action. Mary told the disciples about the open tomb, and then Peter and the other disciple set out and went toward the tomb. The two were running together, but the other disciple outran Peter.

The other disciple? Who's that? Oh yes, John. And John outran Peter? Is this detail important? It is to John. John wants you to know that he can run faster than Peter! And then he adds that he reached the tomb first.

Of course. John outran Peter, and so, as you do when you're faster, he reached the tomb first. The details are so telling, aren't they?

John continues with the story, telling us that he bent down to look in and saw the linen wrappings lying there, but he did not go in. Then Simon Peter came, following him.

Why was Peter following him? Oh yeah, that's right, as we all know he was following him and showed up later because he's just not as fast a runner as John. Peter, John wants us to know, went into the tomb. He saw the linen wrappings lying there, and the cloth that had been on Jesus' head, not lying with the linen wrappings but rolled up in a place by itself. Then the other disciple, who reached the tomb first— Really, John? You have to remind us again that you got there first? But John saves the best for the end, telling us that he also went in, and he saw and believed …

He saw and believed. As opposed to that infidel Peter. Who also, in case you didn't know, got there second.

(While we're at it, a bit about the Bible: You'll often hear the Bible referred to as God's word. Which can be powerful, to say the least. But this conviction about the Bible being God's word can often lead people to miss the truth that before the Bible is anything else, it is first and foremost a library of stories and poems and letters and accounts written by real people in real places at real times. It's a human word first. Written by flawed, funky, funny people with hangups and agendas and opinions and biases and at times the tremendous need to let you know that they can run faster than that other guy ...)

So now, back to Jesus and Peter having breakfast and Peter looking over his shoulder at John and asking, What about him?

Peter is doing here on the beach what he and John have apparently been doing for a while now—competing, comparing, measuring themselves against each other. And in this sacred, holy moment between Peter and Jesus, when Jesus is essentially saying to Peter, I want you to lead my church, Peter is not think-ing about the massive responsibility he's just been given, he's thinking about ... John.

Which leads us to the line Jesus adds just before the "What is that to you?" question, the line about "If I want him to remain alive until I return ..."

Don't get distracted by this line, looking for some hidden meaning about Jesus' plans or the future of the world or the apoc-alypse or whatever.

I think he's being funny.

He's trying to get across to Peter how insane it is for Peter in this moment to be worried about John. Jesus has something differ-ent for John to do. Peter has his path, John has his.

It's as if Jesus says, If I want monkeys to shoot out his nose, then that's what will happen.

That sort of thing. What Jesus says here is absurd because Peter's asking about John in this moment is absurd.

It's as if he's saying, Peter, you have your path and John has his path and everybody else each has their own path. It is a tragic waste of your sacred, God-given energies to be looking over your shoulder wondering about his path when you have your own path, and it isn't his or hers or theirs or anyone else's, and to be true to your path will take every single ounce of energy you have. I have work for you to do in the world, and when you're distracted with someone else's work, you miss out on your work, your life, your joy.

As a pastor for over 20 years, I can't begin to count how many times I've interacted with someone about their life and their calling and their path, only to have them talk about someone else's path, or someone else's expectations for them, someone else's talent or ability or opportunity.

Which takes me back to the enduring power and grace of this question Jesus asks. In those moments when I'm distracted from my own path, looking over my shoulder, wondering about someone else's path, I'm reminded of the words of Jesus, the question of Jesus, asking me, What is that to you?

Because the answer for Peter is then the same answer that it's always been for me, and for you.

Nothing.

Rob Bell *is a pastor, teacher and New York* Times *best-selling author.*

ACKNOWLEDGMENTS

This book exists only thanks to its countless champions, and I find I must end a book of questions with one of my own—how can I ever thank you all?

To my editors at TIME—Nancy Gibbs, who dreamed up this project and who entrusts me with the best beat in journalism, and Michael Duffy and Michael Scherer, who have taught me to report with integrity and continue to push me to write with grace. To my colleagues and friends in TIME's Washington bureau, for your constant insight, shared with the best mix of brilliance and laughter.

To Time Inc. Books—Steve Koepp, who always thinks of how to best serve the reader, and Roe D'Angelo, who encouraged me to take on this project and whose editorial ingenuity and wit held together every single bit. Special thanks to Gina Scauzillo, who doggedly managed every detail of a complicated contract and payment process, secured all necessary rights and made sure all our contributors were paid; Anne-Michelle Gallero, who handled the design process; and Courtney Mifsud, who coordinated contracts and payments and tracked everything in spreadsheets extraordinaire. And to Gary Stewart, who designed our cover and brought beauty to the pages that followed.

To each of this collection's contributors—your enthusiasm along the way has given me great heart. Thank you for inviting me to share in your imaginations and discoveries, and for joining with TIME to inspire the world to question anew. And to the teams behind each contributor, including Edwin Banacia, Kevin Birmingham, John Chryssavgis, Ken Gavin, Alex Karloutsos, Velvet Kelm, Chieko Noguchi, Lina Plath, A. Larry Ross, Ed Thornton, Mark Withoos, Joseph Zwilling and more.

To my friends and family—doing life together is my spice and joy. To my father Jeff, whose passion for education and nature has enriched my ability to question. To my Jenkins women—I cannot imagine a stronger, more inspirational group—to my grandmother Peg, whose spark and courage provide daily wisdom, and to my aunts Cilla, Cindy and Deborah, who compel me to seek to love.

To my sister Rebecca, you are my fiercest friend, the purest heart and my forever favorite. I want to be like you when I grow up. And to my beautiful mother Robin, who every morning that I can remember has lit a candle to waken the dawn and read the Scriptures in her kitchen rocking chair. Your love has given me the world.

Elizabeth

Jesus' Questions In Their Scriptural Context

LISTED BY PAGE

---•••---

1. *If you love those who love you, what reward will you get?*
(MATTHEW 5:46)
Jesus is addressing the crowds and the disciples in his Sermon on the Mount.

5. *Can any one of you by worrying add a single hour to your life?*
(MATTHEW 6:27)
Jesus is addressing the crowds and the disciples in his Sermon on the Mount.

9. *Why do you see the speck in your neighbor's eye, but do not notice the log in your own eye?* (MATTHEW 7:3, NRSV)
Jesus is addressing the crowds and the disciples in his Sermon on the Mount.

13. *You of little faith, why are you so afraid?* (MATTHEW 8:26)
Jesus and the disciples are on a boat in the Sea of Galilee when a furious storm begins. Jesus is asleep and the disciples wake him, saying, "Lord, save us! We're going to drown!"

17. *Do you believe that I am able to do this?* (MATTHEW 9:28)
After Jesus raises a girl from the dead, two blind men follow him and call out, "Have mercy on us, Son of David!"

22. *What did you go out into the wilderness to see?* (MATTHEW 11:7)
Jesus speaks to the crowds about John the Baptist, who is imprisoned.

26. *If any of you has a sheep and it falls into a pit on the Sabbath, will you not take hold of it and lift it out?* (MATTHEW 12:11)
Jesus is in a synagogue with a man whose hand is shriveled. The Pharisees, religious leaders of the day, question Jesus about healing on the Sabbath.

30. *Who is my mother, and who are my brothers?* (MATTHEW 12:48)
Jesus is told that his mother and brothers are outside and want to speak with him while he is teaching.

33. *Why did you doubt?* (MATTHEW 14:31)
Shortly before dawn, Jesus walks on the Sea of Galilee toward his disciples in a boat. He calls to Peter, who walks on the water toward Jesus and then begins to sink when he sees the wind.

37. *Why do you break the command of God for the sake of your tradition?*
(MATTHEW 15:3)
Jesus is speaking with the Pharisees and teachers of the law who
came from Jerusalem.

41. *What good will it be for someone to gain the whole world, yet forfeit their
soul?* (MATTHEW 16:26)
Jesus has just explained to his disciples that he must go to
Jerusalem and be killed and raised to life. Peter rebukes him, and
Jesus replies, "Get behind me, Satan!"

45. *If a man owns a hundred sheep, and one of them wanders away, will he
not leave the ninety-nine on the hills and go to look for the one that wandered
off?* (MATTHEW 18:12)
Jesus is teaching his disciples in parables.

48. *Haven't you read that at the beginning the Creator "made them male and
female"?* (MATTHEW 19:4)
The Pharisees in Judea have just asked Jesus whether divorce is
lawful. Jesus is about to ask the children to come unto him

52. *Why do you ask me about what is good?* (MATTHEW 19:17)
A man has just asked Jesus, "What good thing must I do to get
eternal life?"

56. *Which is greater: the gold, or the temple that makes the gold sacred?*
(MATTHEW 23:17)
Jesus has entered Jerusalem on a donkey and is teaching in the
temple courts.

60. *Why are you bothering this woman?* (MATTHEW 26:10)
Jesus is in Bethany, at the home of Simon the Leper, when a
woman with an alabaster jar pours expensive ointment on his
head. The disciples are indignant at the extravagance.

64. *Do you think I cannot call on my Father, and he will at once put at my
disposal more than twelve legions of angels?* (MATTHEW 26:53)
In the Garden of Gethsemane after the Last Supper, Jesus is
arrested. One of his disciples cuts off the ear of the servant of
the high priest.

68. *My God, my God, why have you forsaken me?* (MATTHEW 27:46)
Jesus hangs on the cross on Golgotha.

72. *Which is easier: to say to this paralyzed man, "Your sins are forgiven," or
to say, "Get up, take your mat and walk"?* (MARK 2:9)
In Capernaum, men lower a paralyzed man to Jesus through a
roof. Jesus forgives his sins, and teachers of the law wonder why
he speaks the way he does.

76. *How can the guests of the bridegroom fast while he is with them?*
(MARK 2:19)
John the Baptist's disciples and the Pharisees are fasting, and a
group wonders why Jesus' followers are not.

80. *Which is lawful on the Sabbath: to do good or to do evil, to save life or to
kill?* (MARK 3:4)
Jesus heals a man with a shriveled hand in a synagogue on the
Sabbath.

84. *How can Satan drive out Satan?* (MARK 3:23)
The crowd following Jesus was so large that he and the disciples
could not eat in a house. Teachers of the law from Jerusalem said,
"By the prince of demons he is driving out demons."

89. *What is your name?* (MARK 5:9)
When Jesus arrives in Gerasenes, a man with an impure spirit
falls on his knees before him. Jesus calls the spirits out of the
man and gives them permission to go into a herd of pigs.

93. *Who touched my clothes?* (MARK 5:30)
Jesus is en route to heal Jairus' daughter when a woman who had
bled for 12 years touches his cloak and is healed.

96. *Why all this commotion and wailing?* (MARK 5:39)
Jesus arrives at the home of Jairus, a synagogue leader whose
daughter has just died.

100. *Don't you see that nothing that enters a person from the outside can
defile them?* (MARK 7:18)
The Pharisees see Jesus' disciples eating food from unwashed
hands and ask why they didn't follow the tradition of the elders.
Later, the disciples ask about Jesus' reply.

105. *Why does this generation ask for a sign?* (MARK 8:12)
After Jesus feeds 4,000 people with seven loaves of bread and a
few small fish, the Pharisees ask him for a sign from heaven.

110. *Why are you talking about having no bread?* (MARK 8:17)
Jesus addresses his disciples, who had forgotten to bring bread, except for one loaf they already had, on the boat.

116. *Who do people say I am?* (MARK 8:27)
On the way to Caesarea Philippi, Jesus speaks with his disciples.

120. *How long has he been like this?* (MARK 9:21)
After the transfiguration, a man brings Jesus his son, who collapses on the ground and foams at the mouth and gnashes his teeth.

124. *How can you make it salty again?* (MARK 9:50)
Jesus teaches his disciples in Capernaum.

128. *Why do you call me good?* (MARK 10:18)
A man runs up to Jesus and falls on his knees before him. "Good teacher," he asks, "what must I do to inherit eternal life?"

132. *Can you drink the cup I drink or be baptized with the baptism I am baptized with?* (MARK 10:38)
James and John, sons of Zebedee, ask Jesus to let them sit at his right and left hand in his glory.

135. *What do you want me to do for you?* (MARK 10:51)
As Jesus and his disciples are leaving the city of Jericho, Bartimaeus, a blind man begging on the roadside, calls out to Jesus. "Jesus, Son of David, have mercy on me!" he cries.

139. *John's baptism—was it from heaven, or of human origin?*
(MARK 11:30)
Jesus is walking in the temple courts in Jerusalem when the chief
priests and elders begin to question him.

143. *Haven't you read this passage of Scripture?* (MARK 12:10)
Jesus speaks in parables about a man who planted a vineyard and
sent various emissaries to collect the fruit.

147. *Whose image is this? And whose inscription?* (MARK 12:16)
Jesus examines a denarius, a coin, when the Pharisees and
Herodians ask Jesus about paying the imperial tax to Caesar.

151. *Simon, are you asleep? Couldn't you keep watch for one hour?*
(MARK 14:37)
In the Garden of Gethsemane, Jesus prays. His disciples Peter,
James and John fall asleep.

155. *Am I leading a rebellion that you have come out with swords and clubs
to capture me?* (MARK 14:48)
Jesus is arrested in Gethsemane, and someone cuts off the ear of
the servant of the high priest.

159. *Why were you searching for me? Didn't you know I had to be in my
Father's house?* (LUKE 2:49)
After Passover in Jerusalem, Jesus stays behind when his parents
leave, unaware that he isn't with them. His parents return to
Jerusalem in search of him.

163. *Can the blind lead the blind?* (LUKE 6:39)
Jesus teaches in parables.

167. *Why do you call me, "Lord, Lord," and do not do what I say?* (LUKE 6:46)
Jesus teaches in parables.

170. *Do you see this woman?* (LUKE 7:44)
As Jesus sits at a Pharisee's table, a woman washes his feet with her tears, wipes them with her hair and pours perfume on them.

173. *Which of these three, do you think, proved neighbor to the man who fell among the robbers?* (LUKE 10:36, RSV)
Jesus concludes the parable of the Good Samaritan.

177. *Which of you fathers, if your son asks for a fish, will give him a snake instead?* (LUKE 11:11)
Jesus has just taught the disciples how to pray.

181. *Do you think that these Galileans were worse sinners than all the other Galileans because they suffered this way?* (LUKE 13:2)
People have just told Jesus about Galileans whose blood Pilate has mixed with sacrifices.

184. *What is the kingdom of God like? What shall I compare it to?* (LUKE 13:18)
Jesus tells parables of the Kingdom of God.

188. *Or suppose a woman has ten silver coins and loses one. Doesn't she light a lamp, sweep the house and search carefully until she finds it?* (LUKE 15:8)
Jesus tells parables to the Pharisees and the teachers of the law.

192. *Were not all ten cleansed? Where are the other nine? Has no one returned to give praise to God except the foreigner?* (LUKE 17:17–18)
Jesus heals 10 men with leprosy on his way to Jerusalem, along the border between Samaria and Galilee.

196. *When the Son of Man comes, will he find faith on the earth?* (LUKE 18:8)
Jesus tells his disciples a parable about a widow who continued to ask a judge for justice.

200. *For who is greater, the one who is at the table or the one who serves?* (LUKE 22:27)
At the Last Supper, a dispute arises among the disciples as to who is considered to be the greatest.

204. *Judas, are you betraying the Son of Man with a kiss?* (LUKE 22:48)
Jesus is arrested.

208. *Why are you troubled?* (LUKE 24:38)
Jesus appears to the disciples after his resurrection. They think they see a ghost.

212. *What do you want?* (JOHN 1:38)
Two of John the Baptist's followers follow Jesus when he passes by.

216. *Woman, why do you involve me?* (JOHN 2:4)
At a wedding, Jesus' mother tells him the wine has run out.

220. *Do you not understand these things?* (JOHN 3:10)
Nicodemus, a member of the Jewish ruling council, comes to Jesus at night and inquires, "How can someone be born when they are old?"

223. *Will you give me a drink?* (JOHN 4:7)
Jesus sits at Jacob's well in Samaria while his disciples are gone, and a Samaritan woman arrives to draw water.

227. *Do you want to be healed?* (JOHN 5:6, ESV)
At the pool of Bethesda in Jerusalem, Jesus speaks with a man who had been an invalid for 38 years.

231. *Does this offend you?* (JOHN 6:61)
Jesus is teaching at a synagogue in Capernaum.

235. *You do not want to leave, too, do you?* (JOHN 6:67)
When other followers turn away from Jesus after hard teachings, Jesus turns to his disciples.

239. *Woman, where are they? Has no one condemned you?* (JOHN 8:10)
Teachers of the law bring a woman caught in adultery to Jesus in the temple courts. "Let any one of you who is without sin be the first to throw a stone at her," he says.

243. *What shall I say? "Father, save me from this hour"?* (JOHN 12:27)
Jesus has entered Jerusalem, when the crowd greeted him with palm branches and cries of "Hosanna."

248. *Do you understand what I have done for you?* (JOHN 13:12)
Jesus has just washed his disciples' feet during their final
Passover together.

250. *Will you really lay down your life for me?* (JOHN 13:38)
Jesus has given his disciples a new commandment: "As I have
loved you, so you must love one another." Peter asks why he can't
follow Jesus now.

254. *My Father's house has many rooms; if that were not so, would I have
told you that I am going there to prepare a place for you?* (JOHN 14:2)
Jesus comforts his disciples about the future.

258. *Who is it you want?* (JOHN 18:4,7)
Judas, soldiers and religious leaders arrive to arrest Jesus.

262. *Shall I not drink the cup the Father has given me?* (JOHN 18:11)
Peter cuts off the high priest's servant's right ear, and Jesus tells
him to put his sword away.

266. *Why question me?* (JOHN 18:21)
The high priest questions Jesus about his disciples and teaching.

268. *Woman, why are you weeping? Who is it you are looking for?*
(JOHN 20:15)
After his resurrection, Jesus appears to Mary Magdalene, who is
outside the tomb, crying.

272. *Friends, haven't you any fish?* (JOHN 21:5)
Jesus appears to his disciples by the Sea of Galilee after his resurrection. They do not recognize him.

276. *Simon, son of John, do you love me?* (JOHN 21:17)
When the disciples finish eating, Jesus asks Simon this question three times.

279. *If I want him to remain alive until I return, what is that to you?* (JOHN 21:22)
Peter turns and sees the disciple whom Jesus loved following them. "Lord, what about him?" he asks.